The Tribal Mirror:
Why We're All
a Little Narcissistic
(and How We Can Save
Ourselves From Ourselves)

The Tribal Mirror:
Why We're All
a Little Narcissistic
(and How We Can Save
Ourselves From Ourselves)

Rex Nihilo

Copyright Page

Title: *The Tribal Mirror: Why We're All a Little Narcissistic (and How We Can Save Ourselves From Ourselves)*

Author: *Rex Nihilo*

For information, permission requests, or media inquiries, contact:
Quite Frank Educational Services
Richmond, BC, Canada

Cover design by the author.
Printed in the United States of America.

ISBN: 978-1-997668-58-9

Library and Archives Canada Cataloguing in Publication Data pending.

Publisher's Note

This book represents the author's independent research and reflection. The opinions expressed are those of the author and do not necessarily reflect the views of Quite Frank Educational Services or any affiliated organization.

The Tribal Mirror: Why We're All a Little Narcissistic (and How We Can Save Ourselves From Ourselves)

Table of Contents

Desmond Tutu – *"My humanity is bound up in yours, for we can only be human together."* (*No Future Without Forgiveness*, 1999)

Jonathan Haidt – *"Morality binds and blinds. It binds us into teams, but it blinds us to the fact that each team is composed of good people who have something important to say."* (*The Righteous Mind*, 2012)

Gordon Allport – *"The familiar is readily accepted; the unfamiliar tends to be rejected."* (*The Nature of Prejudice*, 1954)

Robin Dunbar – *"Our capacity for friendship is not infinite; it is limited by the size of our brain."* (*How Many Friends Does One Person Need?*, 2010)

Jamil Zaki – *"Empathy is not a fixed trait, like eye color. It's a skill, like learning to speak a language or play a sport."* (*The War for Kindness*, 2019)

Sherry Turkle – *"Technology doesn't just change what we do; it changes who we are."* (*Alone Together*, 2011)

Disclaimer

This book is intended for educational and informational purposes only. It is not a substitute for professional advice in psychology, medicine, or any other field. Readers are encouraged to seek qualified professional guidance when making decisions that may affect their mental health, relationships, or wellbeing.

While every effort has been made to ensure the accuracy and reliability of the information presented, the author and publisher make no warranties or guarantees and accept no responsibility for any errors or omissions. Any examples, anecdotes, or humor used throughout the text are intended for illustration and entertainment and should not be taken as literal accounts of real individuals unless otherwise noted.

AI Acknowledgment

This book was created through a collaborative process between the author and advanced AI tools. Artificial intelligence was used to assist in **researching source material, structuring chapters, editing drafts, and refining tone and style**. The final content, themes, and direction were shaped by the author, Rex Nihilo.

This acknowledgment is included in the spirit of transparency, reflecting the evolving nature of authorship and the creative possibilities of human–AI collaboration.

Introduction

Imagine this: you're at a family barbecue. The food is great, the drinks are flowing, and then—inevitably—someone brings up politics. Suddenly, Uncle Joe is red in the face, Aunt Mary is quoting something she read on Facebook (with great conviction but zero fact-checking), and your cousin is googling whether moving to New Zealand is still an option.

If this sounds familiar, congratulations—you've experienced **social narcissism** up close.

It's not just your family, of course. Zoom out from the backyard to the wider world, and you'll find entire nations, political parties, religions, and even sports fans locked in the same pattern: "We're right, they're wrong, and the fact they don't recognize our greatness is an outrage." If you've ever wondered why humanity, with all its science and Netflix subscriptions, still struggles with petty tribal squabbles, the answer lies deep in our evolutionary wiring.

You see, we didn't evolve to thrive in globalized societies of eight billion people. Our ancestors lived in small groups, maybe 150 people tops—the size of a modest wedding guest list. In that world, survival depended on fierce loyalty to your tribe. "Us" meant protection, food, and trust. "Them" meant danger, competition, and sometimes outright warfare. Those instincts were once useful. Today, they're like carrying a stone axe to a Wi-Fi café: charming in theory, disastrous in practice.

This book is about what happens when those tribal instincts collide with the modern world. Psychologists call the toxic version **collective narcissism**: a fragile, defensive belief that your group is not only special but unfairly unrecognized. Think of it as group-level insecurity with a megaphone. It explains everything from Twitter flame wars to international conflicts, from partisan politics to why your neighbor thinks their favorite sports team is morally superior to yours.

But here's the twist: our greatest hope lies in the very same social brain that got us into this mess. Yes, we're wired for tribalism, but we're also wired for empathy, storytelling, and cooperation. History shows that societies have, at their best, built remarkable systems for reconciliation and understanding. From South Africa's Truth and Reconciliation Commission to the Good Friday Agreement in Northern Ireland, humanity has shown that it can sometimes outgrow its worst instincts.

This book will take you on a tour of the science, history, and everyday comedy of being human. You'll meet brainy monkeys, insecure tribes, conspiracy theories in the wild, and empathy's strange double life as both peacemaker and troublemaker. Along the way, we'll keep it light, because frankly, nothing is more human than laughing at our own absurdities—even while we're trying to fix them.

By the end, you'll not only understand why humans seem doomed to repeat the same tribal dramas—you'll also discover the tools we already have to escape them. Not by erasing our tribes, but by practicing what I like to call **"enlightened tribalism"**: belonging without belligerence, pride without fragility, and strong communities that don't need enemies to thrive.

So grab a plate, sit down at the barbecue table of human history, and let's figure out how to stop flipping the picnic table every time we disagree. Spoiler alert: it starts with listening, and yes, that means Uncle Joe too.

Chapter 1: Why Humans Are Basically Group Projects with Legs

If you've ever suffered through a group project in school, you already know the essence of the human condition. One person does all the work, another takes credit, someone else mysteriously disappears halfway through, and at least one member spends the whole time arguing about font choices on the PowerPoint slides.

That, in a nutshell, is humanity: a species designed for teamwork, yet constantly frustrated by the very people we depend on.

It may not sound flattering, but evolution didn't build us to be lone wolves, nor did it make us rugged individualists. It built us to be cooperative primates—essentially, group projects with legs. Our survival, from the very beginning, has depended on whether we could get along (well enough) with others, share food, keep watch for predators, and occasionally avoid hitting each other with sticks when we disagreed.

The Lone Caveman Problem

Let's run a quick thought experiment. Picture an early human—let's call him Ogg—deciding one day that he's had enough of tribal drama. He's sick of sharing mammoth steaks, tired of listening to the chief's motivational speeches, and definitely over the endless cave debates about whether fire should be communal property.

So Ogg storms off in protest, vowing to start his own tribe of one. He sets out across the savannah with nothing but a stick, a half-eaten root, and his misplaced confidence.

How does Ogg do? Spoiler: not great.

- Without his tribe, he can't defend against predators. Lions aren't impressed by his stick.

- He can't hunt effectively alone. Try taking down a bison solo with Stone Age tools—Ogg might as well have brought a salad fork.

- He's vulnerable to illness and injury. Twist an ankle while foraging? Congratulations, Ogg—you've just become lunch.

The moral of Ogg's short and unhappy life: humans are not designed to function solo. Survival requires allies.

The Social Brain: Big Heads, Bigger Drama

This reality shaped our very biology. Evolution decided that if humans were going to survive, our brains needed an upgrade—not in tool-making first, but in gossip management.

Enter the **Social Brain Hypothesis**, proposed by anthropologist Robin Dunbar. The gist is simple but mind-blowing: the reason primates (including us) have such large brains isn't just to outsmart predators or invent wheels, but to handle the dizzying complexity of social life.

Think of it this way: it's one thing to remember where the fruit trees are. It's another thing entirely to remember that Grunk owes you a favor because you covered his shift on mammoth duty, while also remembering that Lina is mad at Torg because he stole her berries, and meanwhile, half the tribe suspects the shaman of hogging mushrooms.

The mental gymnastics required to juggle alliances, grudges, obligations, and gossip—that's what expanded the neocortex. Human survival wasn't just about brute strength or sharp tools; it was about keeping track of who was sleeping with whom, who could be trusted, and who was about to stab you in the back (literally or figuratively).

In other words, your brain is basically a soap opera manager.

Dunbar's Number: Why You're Maxed Out at 150 Friends

Dunbar's research didn't stop with "our brains are big because we like drama." He also proposed a famous limit, now known as **Dunbar's Number**: the maximum number of stable, meaningful relationships a human can maintain is about **150**.

This doesn't mean you can't *know* more than 150 people. You might have 2,000 Facebook friends or follow 700 people on Instagram. But meaningful connection—the kind where you not only know someone's name but also how they connect to others in your circle—tops out at around 150.

Archaeologists have found this number reflected everywhere:

- The typical size of Neolithic villages.

- The standard structure of Roman military units.

- Even the maximum size of modern companies before they tend to split into smaller sub-units.

It's as if human society has an internal "memory card" that starts flashing "storage full" at 151.

Think about your own life: if you try to invite every single person you've ever met to your wedding, it won't just be financially ruinous—it'll be cognitively impossible. Your brain simply wasn't built to manage a wedding guest list beyond 150.

This limit, charming as it sounds, has massive consequences. It explains why we gravitate toward **tribes**—manageable circles of trust and familiarity. Anything beyond that, and we default to lumping people into categories. Which leads us to the most notorious feature of our group-project brains: the **us vs. them problem**.

Why "Us vs. Them" is Baked into Our Brains

Evolutionary psychology tells us that forming an "in-group" and an "out-group" wasn't a bug—it was a feature. Our ancestors didn't have the luxury of considering all of humanity as one big family. They needed to know, quickly and decisively: Who's with us, and who's against us?

This shortcut made survival efficient. If someone was from your tribe, odds were they were safe. If someone was from another tribe, odds were they wanted your food, your land, or your spouse.

Today, the consequences are everywhere:

- Sports rivalries ("Yankees fans are the worst").

- Political polarization ("the other party wants to ruin the country").

- Even neighborhood disputes ("people from *that* street never mow their lawns").

The us-vs-them instinct once protected us. Now it mostly fuels Facebook arguments.

The Group Project Curse

Here's the funny thing: for all our tribal instincts, humans are actually spectacularly bad at cooperating smoothly. We need groups to survive, but we also drive each other insane in groups.

Anthropologists point out that cooperation required two big innovations:

1. **Punishing freeloaders** — early tribes had to figure out how to deal with Ogg when he skipped mammoth duty but still showed up for dinner.

2. **Rewarding generosity** — people who shared meat or resources gained prestige, which boosted their status (and, let's be honest, their dating prospects).

In other words, humanity's first "currencies" weren't coins or beads—they were **reputation and trust**. If you were selfish or unreliable, your tribe didn't just glare at you—they might exile you, which was a death sentence.

This ancient reality still haunts us in modern "group projects":

- At work, when someone slacks off on a team project, everyone else seethes, even if the actual material cost is small.

- In families, one sibling who doesn't help care for an elderly parent often becomes the target of group resentment.

- In politics, free-rider accusations ("you're not pulling your weight") are some of the most powerful tools of persuasion—or vilification.

The group project never ended. It just evolved into every aspect of society.

Your Brain: Half Soap Opera, Half Spreadsheet

So, to recap:

- Humans are wired for groups.

- Our brains got bigger not for hunting, but for managing gossip and alliances.

- We max out at 150 meaningful relationships.

- We instinctively divide the world into "us" and "them."

- Cooperation is essential, but also maddening.

All of this points to a strange but profound truth: **we are both brilliant and ridiculous as a species.** Brilliant because cooperation allowed us to build civilizations, invent Wi-Fi, and land on the moon. Ridiculous because we still squabble like cavemen over berries, except now the berries are Twitter blue checkmarks.

This double-edged nature of our tribal wiring is the foundation for everything else in this book. Understanding why we're group projects with legs explains why collective narcissism arises, why empathy fails across divides, and why history is filled with both breathtaking cooperation and catastrophic conflict.

Back to Ogg

Before we close this chapter, let's return to Ogg—the caveman who thought he could go it alone. Predictably, Ogg didn't last long in the wilderness. But his story doesn't end with his bones being picked clean by hyenas. His short-lived rebellion gave his tribe a valuable lesson: cooperation wasn't optional, it was survival.

His cousins, watching his failure, stuck closer together. They shared food, punished freeloaders, swapped stories around the fire, and in doing so, shaped the very psychology that lives in us today.

We are Ogg's descendants, but hopefully a little wiser. We still crave tribes, we still obsess over fairness in group projects, and we still roll our eyes at freeloaders. But unlike Ogg, we now face a world of eight billion people—a project so massive that it makes "150" look laughably quaint.

The big question is: can a species built for small tribes figure out how to work together on a global group project—without setting the PowerPoint on fire?

That, dear reader, is the story we're about to explore.

Chapter 2: Dunbar's Number and the 150-Person Problem

If you've ever tried to organize a wedding, you already know what Robin Dunbar discovered after years of research: there is a hard limit to how many people you can keep track of before your brain simply throws up its hands and says, "Nope."

The average couple, armed with spreadsheets, color-coded seating charts, and the combined patience of saints, soon discovers the *wedding paradox*: no matter how carefully you plan, someone's Great Aunt Mildred is going to get stuck at the table with your old college roommate, and your father-in-law is going to demand why "those people" are sitting so close to the cake.

This chaos isn't a personal failure. It's not even about family politics (though that certainly doesn't help). It's biology. Your brain has a natural cap on how many meaningful relationships it can handle, and that number is roughly **150**.

That's **Dunbar's Number**, and once you understand it, the world makes a lot more sense.

The Math of Belonging

Robin Dunbar, a British anthropologist with a knack for noticing patterns, started by studying primates. He found something curious: species with bigger brains lived in bigger social groups. Chimpanzees, baboons, gorillas—all followed this rule.

So Dunbar asked: what about humans? If you take the size of our neocortex and run the numbers, what's the predicted group size for Homo sapiens?

Answer: **about 150.**

Not 15, not 1,500—just 150. That's the maximum number of relationships you can realistically maintain where you not only know people individually, but also how they all connect to each other.

Think of it as the "soap opera limit": you can only keep track of so many characters before the plotlines become impossible to follow. Beyond 150, you lose the ability to remember who betrayed whom, who owes whom a favor, and who's secretly dating the chief's daughter.

Villages, Armies, and Start-Ups

What makes Dunbar's Number so fascinating is how it appears *everywhere* across history and culture.

- **Neolithic villages**: Archaeological evidence shows ancient farming communities consistently hovered around 120–160 people. Beyond that size, they tended to split into new settlements.

- **Roman armies**: A basic fighting unit, the "century," wasn't 100 men, despite the name—it averaged around 150. Apparently, the Romans knew what Google project managers now know: once a group gets bigger than that, productivity tanks.

- **Amish communities**: Many Amish settlements split once they reach about 150 members. It's not about theology; it's about social cohesion.

- **Modern companies**: Business researchers have found that organizations often restructure or splinter at around—you guessed it—150 employees. That's when bureaucracy creeps in, and suddenly someone decides you need an HR department.

Even today, the echoes of Dunbar's Number are everywhere:

- The average number of people you can keep in your phone contacts *and actually remember who they are.*

- The number of regulars a barista can recognize by name and order before resorting to "uh, latte guy."

- The number of "close friends" most people report across cultures.

It's as if our brains come preloaded with 150 slots for meaningful connections, like an old-school Rolodex.

Facebook vs. The Human Brain

This is where Dunbar's Number runs headfirst into the modern world. Social media platforms are built on the idea that **more is better**: more friends, more followers, more connections.

But here's the catch: having 2,000 Facebook "friends" doesn't mean you can actually maintain 2,000 relationships. You still only have bandwidth for about 150 people. The rest are social wallpaper.

Studies of social media use show that even heavy Facebook users only interact regularly with about 150 people. Everyone else is just part of the digital crowd—faces in the hallway of your online high school, vaguely familiar but ultimately unmanageable.

This explains why online networks can feel both massive and lonely. You may be "connected" to thousands, but your brain can only truly keep track of a small circle. The rest? They're just guest stars in your mental soap opera, destined to be forgotten after a few episodes.

The Concentric Circles of Connection

Of course, not all relationships are equal. Dunbar refined his theory to include *layers* of intimacy, like the rings of a tree:

- **5 people:** Your innermost circle—the ones you'd call if you accidentally murdered someone and needed help hiding the body. (Not that you should. But still.)

- **15 people:** Your close friends. The ones you'd lend money to without too much worry.

- **50 people:** Your good friends. You know their birthdays, their kids' names, and their food allergies.

- **150 people:** Your stable social circle. The people you'd invite to a big life event, like a wedding.

- **500 people:** Your acquaintances. You know their face, might wave in passing, but wouldn't loan them $5.

- **1,500 people:** The limit of the number of people you can even *recognize*.

This layering explains why we feel stretched thin when we try to maintain too many relationships at once. Humans are meant to concentrate energy on a small, inner circle, while still holding looser ties with a broader group.

In modern terms: your five besties get daily text messages; your 50 "good friends" get Christmas cards; your 150 get wedding invites; your 500 get Facebook likes; and your 1,500 get vague nods in the grocery store.

Why the Limit Matters

Dunbar's Number isn't just trivia. It has profound implications for society.

1. **Trust and cohesion:** Groups under 150 tend to self-regulate. Everyone knows each other's reputation, so freeloaders can't hide. Beyond that size, anonymity creeps in—and so does crime, corruption, and bureaucracy.

2. **Politics and identity**: In small groups, politics is personal—
   everyone knows the leader. In large groups, politics becomes
   abstract. That's when "us vs. them" narratives become necessary to
   maintain cohesion. (More on this in the next chapter.)

3. **Loneliness epidemic**: In a world of sprawling cities and digital
   networks, many people feel isolated because their inner circles are
   shrinking. We're surrounded by strangers but lack the 150-strong
   support networks our brains expect.

The Soap Opera Test

Here's a fun way to test Dunbar's Number in your own life: list the people
whose interpersonal drama you actively follow. Not just "I know them," but
"I know who they're dating, what they're stressed about, and how they feel
about pineapple on pizza."

Chances are, it'll cap out around 150. That's your personal soap opera cast.
Everyone else is a background extra—nice enough, but not relevant to the
plot.

This test also explains why office gossip spreads so quickly in workplaces
under 150. Everyone knows everyone else, so the social web is tight. Once a
workplace grows beyond that, gossip loses its power because people don't
know each other well enough to care.

Weddings, Funerals, and the Dunbar Effect

Life milestones often reveal the 150-person cap. Weddings, funerals,
graduations—these are moments when you try to gather "everyone
important." And guess what? The number almost always hovers around
Dunbar's Number.

- **Weddings**: Average guest list size in many cultures is ~150. Coincidence? Nope.

- **Funerals**: Anthropologists have found that funeral attendance often falls in the same range, reflecting the deceased's stable network.

- **Graduations/parties**: Big enough to invite all your "meaningful connections," small enough not to collapse into chaos.

The brain's natural limit shapes not just our relationships, but our rituals.

When 150 Breaks Down

Of course, not all groups respect the limit. Governments, corporations, even social clubs often balloon far beyond it. When they do, they need new tools to maintain cohesion:

- **Formal laws and rules** replace gossip and reputation.

- **Bureaucracy** emerges to track obligations and enforce fairness.

- **Symbols and stories** (flags, anthems, team mascots) are invented to hold massive groups together emotionally.

In other words, everything we think of as "civilization" is essentially humanity's workaround for the fact that our brains can't handle more than 150 people. Cities, nations, religions—they're all ways of pretending we're one big tribe when really, our mental wiring is still stuck in village mode.

Why This Sets the Stage for Narcissistic Tribes

Here's where this becomes crucial for our larger story. If humans max out at 150 meaningful relationships, then anyone beyond that number is cognitively filed as "outsider."

That doesn't mean we hate them automatically—but it means they don't trigger the same level of empathy or trust. We care deeply about our inner circle. Beyond that, empathy tapers off.

This cognitive bottleneck is one of the root causes of **collective narcissism**. When groups grow too big to sustain genuine connection, they rely on myths of superiority and grievance to hold themselves together. "We are special" replaces "I know and trust you."

Dunbar's Number isn't just about friendships. It's about the psychological architecture of division. And it's why the next chapter—on the us-vs-them mindset—is where things start to get really interesting (and really messy).

Aunt Mildred's Revenge

Let's circle back to the wedding seating chart, because that's really where this chapter began. You tried to invite everyone who mattered. You maxed out at around 150. You discovered that your brain could juggle only so many dramas, and beyond that, it collapsed into chaos.

And yet, despite your best efforts, Great Aunt Mildred still ended up at the "wrong" table. She glares through the entire dinner. She tells everyone afterward that she was snubbed. She will not forgive you for the rest of your life.

This, too, is part of Dunbar's Number. You can only manage so many relationships at once. Someone always falls through the cracks. And when they do, the whole fragile balance of your tribe gets a little wobbly.

Congratulations: you've just reenacted the human condition.

Chapter 3: Us vs. Them — The Mind's Default Setting

Imagine you're standing in line at the coffee shop, minding your own business, when suddenly a group of tourists comes in wearing matching neon shirts. Within thirty seconds, your brain has already formed an opinion: "They're not from here."

You don't know their names. You don't know their politics. You don't know if they prefer oat milk or whole. But your mind has already hit the big red button labeled **"Not Us."**

This instant, unconscious judgment is a feature, not a bug. It's what psychologists call **social categorization**—and it's one of the oldest survival tricks in the human playbook.

Why Your Brain Is Basically a Sorting Hat

In the Harry Potter universe, the Sorting Hat decides who's Gryffindor, Hufflepuff, Ravenclaw, or Slytherin. In your brain, a similar process happens every time you encounter another human being.

Your mind rapidly, almost instantaneously, decides: **are they one of us or one of them?**

This isn't just cultural prejudice or bad manners—it's a cognitive shortcut. Our ancestors needed quick, life-or-death decisions about strangers. Is that hunter-gatherer approaching us to share berries, or to steal ours? Friend or foe? Ally or rival?

The **sorting mechanism** saved time, reduced risk, and (mostly) worked. Today, it still operates in the background, even though the stakes are usually lower. (The tourist in the neon shirt is unlikely to steal your mammoth meat.)

The Minimal Group Paradigm: Divided by Pie

Psychologists Henri Tajfel and John Turner, back in the 1970s, discovered something both hilarious and terrifying: it takes almost nothing to trigger this us-vs-them mentality.

They ran a now-famous experiment called the **minimal group paradigm.** Participants were randomly assigned to groups based on the flimsiest criteria imaginable—like a coin flip, or which abstract painter they preferred. No shared history. No meaningful difference. Just "Group A" and "Group B."

And yet, once divided, participants consistently favored their own group members. They gave their group more resources, judged them more favorably, and treated the other group with suspicion.

Translation: give humans a pie to split, and we'll find a way to make it tribal. Even if the groups are "People Who Like Triangle Shapes" versus "People Who Like Circles."

In-Group Favoritism: Why We're Nicer to "Us"

Once social categorization kicks in, the next domino is **in-group favoritism**. Simply put, we treat members of our own group more generously and forgivingly than outsiders.

Examples:

- In experiments, people are more likely to share money or food with their in-group.

- We excuse bad behavior from our group ("he's a jerk, but he's *our* jerk").

- We literally process faces from our in-group faster and more accurately at the neurological level.

Think about sports. If your team wins by a shady penalty, you call it "strategy." If the other team does the same thing, it's "cheating." That's in-group favoritism in action.

Or politics: when your party's candidate bends the truth, it's "spin." When the other party's candidate does it, it's "lies."

We're not consistent. We're tribal.

Out-Group Homogeneity: "They're All the Same"

Another quirk of our tribal wiring is the **out-group homogeneity effect.**

This is the tendency to see members of our in-group as unique individuals ("we're all so different and interesting!") while flattening out the identities of outsiders ("they're all the same").

You've seen this play out everywhere:

- Rival fans: "All Yankees fans are obnoxious." Meanwhile, your fellow Red Sox fans are a beautiful mosaic of personalities.

- Politics: "Everyone in that party thinks exactly alike." Meanwhile, your own party contains noble diversity and nuance.

- High school cliques: "The drama kids are all weird." Meanwhile, the athletes are each distinct snowflakes.

The out-group homogeneity effect saves mental energy, but at the cost of accuracy. It paves the way for **stereotyping**—our brain's lazy attempt to summarize strangers with broad, usually negative brushstrokes.

When Favoritism Turns Hostile

Favoring our group is one thing. Actively **derogating** the out-group is another. Unfortunately, it doesn't take much for the first to turn into the second.

Once an out-group is perceived as a threat—competing for resources, blocking goals, or disrespecting our tribe—the tone shifts. What was once indifference turns into antagonism. Suspicion becomes hostility.

At that point, the language changes:

- "They don't get us."

- "They're immoral."

- "They're dangerous."

This escalation is why us-vs-them thinking is so combustible. It starts with favoritism and ends with violence.

An Evolutionary Mismatch

Now, here's the kicker: none of this is a moral failing. It's an evolutionary mismatch.

Our tribal brains evolved in small-scale societies where rapid categorization was useful. In that world, assuming the stranger at the edge of camp was dangerous may have saved lives.

But in a world of eight billion interconnected humans, the same shortcut creates massive dysfunction. The instincts that once protected us now drive prejudice, polarization, and conflict.

Your brain thinks it's still in the savannah, but you're actually at Starbucks arguing about pumpkin spice.

Modern Examples of Tribal Brains at Work

1. **Politics:** Partisan identity has become so fused with personal identity that disagreement feels like personal attack. Democrats and Republicans in the U.S. increasingly see each other not just as rivals, but as existential threats.

2. **Nationalism:** Collective pride turns toxic when it morphs into "our greatness isn't respected." Suddenly, grievances become the national fuel.

3. **Online communities:** Twitter/X, Reddit, Facebook—all amplify tribalism. Each platform becomes an echo chamber where "our side" is always right, and "their side" is always dangerous or stupid.

Everyday Tribal Theater

Let's lighten this up for a second. Tribal brains aren't just behind wars and polarization—they're behind petty everyday nonsense, too.

- Office kitchens: "Marketing never cleans their mugs. Typical."

- Gym culture: "CrossFit people are *all* culty."

- Coffee orders: "People who drink pumpkin spice lattes are basic."

These mini-tribes, while less destructive, are still fueled by the same us-vs-them wiring. Your brain is constantly scanning for cues: who's with me, who's against me, and what does that mean for my place in the group project of life?

Us vs. Them in Your Head

Here's a fun trick: next time you meet someone new, listen to the mental shortcuts firing in your head. You'll notice your brain trying to quickly slot them:

- "Looks like me" → probably safe.

- "Different accent" → not sure.

- "Wearing rival team's jersey" → enemy.

You can catch yourself doing it. The categorization happens in milliseconds, before conscious thought. Recognizing it doesn't erase it, but it's the first step toward managing it.

Why This Matters for What's Coming

So why spend an entire chapter dissecting this default us-vs-them switch? Because it's the foundation of everything that follows.

- Collective narcissism (fragile group pride) grows out of in-group favoritism run amok.

- The empathy gap (caring less for outsiders) is literally built on out-group homogeneity.

- Modern political and cultural divides are just us-vs-them in bigger, louder packaging.

To understand why humanity struggles so badly with polarization, outrage, and conflict, we have to start here—with the little Sorting Hat in our brains, constantly deciding who's "us" and who's "them."

Back to the Coffee Shop

Remember the neon-shirted tourists at the coffee shop? Your brain's Sorting Hat already filed them as "not us." But here's the twist: if you got to know them—shared a table, discovered they love the same TV shows, or realized they also hate pineapple on pizza—your brain would happily refile them into your in-group.

That's the other feature of our tribal wiring: it's flexible. Our "us" can expand. It's not locked at blood relatives or cavemen. We can—and often do—choose new tribes.

The problem is, we rarely take the time. It's easier to trust the Sorting Hat's first judgment than to rewrite the script.

The challenge for humanity is simple, but not easy: can we outgrow our default us-vs-them instincts and build bigger, more inclusive tribes? Or are we doomed to keep dividing ourselves into smaller and smaller factions until no one's left at the wedding but Great Aunt Mildred?

Stay tuned.

Interlude #1: A Day in the Life of a Tribal Brain

Meet Jamie. Jamie is a perfectly ordinary modern human—works in an office, has a smartphone, and owns more reusable grocery bags than any one person really needs. But inside Jamie's head, there's a brain designed for a Stone Age hunter-gatherer tribe. Which makes everyday life... a little weird.

Let's follow Jamie through an average Tuesday and watch how their **tribal brain** hijacks everything.

7:00 AM – The Morning Ritual

Jamie stumbles out of bed and brews coffee. The brain registers this as a sacred tribal ceremony, akin to Stone Age fire-making. Without it, Jamie cannot function. Their inner Ogg mutters: "Without sacred bean water, tribe cannot survive."

When the coffee is ready, the reward system in the brain lights up like a campfire. Dopamine sings. Jamie is now fully prepared for mammoth hunting—or, in this case, replying to emails.

9:00 AM – Enter the Workplace Tribe

Jamie arrives at the office. The open-plan space looks modern, but the brain interprets it as a **tribal camp.** Each department is its own clan:

- **Marketing Tribe:** known for bright clothing and loud laughter.

- **IT Tribe:** live in a mysterious cave filled with wires. They guard the sacred passwords.

- **Finance Tribe:** feared and respected; rumored to hoard numbers like shiny stones.

Jamie's immediate loyalty is to the "Project Team Sub-Tribe." Together, they share resources (coffee pods), form alliances ("I'll cover your meeting if you cover mine"), and grumble about freeloaders (the one guy who always forgets deadlines).

To the tribal brain, this is life or death. Slack messages = tribal signals. Weekly stand-up = council of elders. Budget reviews = ritual sacrifice.

12:30 PM – Foraging Ritual

Jamie and coworkers head to lunch. They could each bring their own food, but the tribal brain insists on eating **together.** Shared meals reinforce bonds. To eat alone at your desk? That's exile. Exile = death.

At the salad bar, Jamie's brain is quietly scanning status signals:

- Who's telling the funniest stories (potential leader material).

- Who's sitting closest to the center of the table (high status).

- Who eats weird food (possible outsider).

It's not snobbery—it's Stone Age pattern recognition, dressed up in business casual.

3:00 PM – The Rival Tribe

An email arrives from "Corporate Headquarters." The tribal brain immediately flags this as communication from an **out-group.**

Jamie's team feels their own importance is under threat. The phrase "synergy initiative" triggers fight-or-flight. Grievances about unfair recognition bubble up: "They don't appreciate us. They never respect our work. They're stealing our resources!"

Congratulations: Jamie's team is now experiencing **collective narcissism.** If someone suggests a conspiracy theory about HQ hiding money in offshore caves, half the team will nod in agreement.

6:00 PM – Ritualized Combat

After work, Jamie goes to the gym. To the tribal brain, this is a display of physical prowess meant to signal fitness to the group. Lifting weights? That's mock hunting. Spinning class? Simulated stampede escape.

Jamie's brain is secretly comparing their performance to others:

- "Am I stronger than that guy?"

- "Do I run faster than her?"

- "Will the tribe admire my sweaty dedication?"

Modern exercise is really Stone Age **status competition** with branded yoga pants.

8:00 PM – The Digital Village Fire

Back home, Jamie scrolls through Twitter. The tribal brain interprets this as **evening campfire gossip.** Except instead of 150 tribe members, it's 1.5 million strangers screaming at each other.

Jamie feels outrage at rival tribes ("How can people believe that nonsense?!") and warm belonging when their own tribe retweets them. Likes = applause around the fire. Retweets = promotion in tribal status.

By 9:00 PM, Jamie is emotionally exhausted, because the tribal brain was never meant to process drama from thousands of strangers in one sitting.

11:00 PM – Sleep, Finally

Jamie lies down. The tribal brain reviews the day:

- Did I maintain alliances?

- Did I defend the tribe from threats?

- Did I increase my status?

- Did I avoid exile?

Satisfied, the brain lets Jamie drift into sleep. Tomorrow, the cycle begins again. Another day of coffee rituals, office clans, rival tribes, and the endless negotiation of belonging.

The Point Beneath the Comedy

The joke here isn't just that Jamie is secretly a caveman in skinny jeans. The deeper truth is this: our brains evolved for **small tribes, gossip fires, and shared hunts.** But we live in a world of megacities, digital networks, and global politics.

That mismatch explains so much of our modern stress:

- Why office politics feel life-or-death.

- Why social media outrage spreads like wildfire.

- Why group projects (whether school, work, or society at large) always feel both essential and maddening.

Jamie is all of us. Every day, we're modern humans running on Stone Age software, navigating a world our brains didn't anticipate.

And unless we understand this wiring, we'll keep letting our tribal brains hijack our global society.

Chapter 4: The Dark Side of Altruism (Part I & II)

Part I: Why Nice Tribes Still Go to War

We like to think of altruism as the warm-and-fuzzy force that makes us human. Sharing food, comforting the sick, babysitting your neighbor's kid—these are the acts that keep communities alive and give us hope for humanity.

But here's the twist: altruism isn't always gentle. In fact, the very instincts that make us care for *our* people are the same ones that can turn us against *other* people.

This paradox is called **parochial altruism**—"parochial" meaning "limited to our own group."

Meat and Murder

Picture a Stone Age tribe gathered around a fire. Everyone is sharing meat from a successful hunt. Children are fed first, elders are respected, and laughter fills the air. This is altruism at its finest: generosity, cooperation, community.

Now, picture what happens when a rival tribe shows up at the edge of the territory. Suddenly, the same loving, generous people are sharpening spears and preparing to bash skulls. Why? Because defending *our* people often means attacking *their* people.

The altruism hasn't disappeared—it's just shifted direction. Protecting and sacrificing for "us" can mean violence toward "them."

Darwin Saw It Coming

Even Charles Darwin, usually remembered for survival of the fittest, recognized this tribal duality. In *The Descent of Man* (1871), he wrote that tribes whose members were "always ready to aid one another, and to sacrifice themselves for the common good" would triumph over less cooperative tribes.

Translation: nice tribes beat selfish tribes. But "nice" here means *nice to each other*, not nice to outsiders.

Darwin, without using the term, was describing parochial altruism.

The Male Warrior Hypothesis

Evolutionary psychologists argue that men, in particular, evolved with a strong bias for group-based aggression. The **Male Warrior Hypothesis** suggests that in ancestral environments, males who banded together to fight rival groups increased their tribe's survival chances.

Traits like bravery, loyalty, and willingness to fight were rewarded—socially and genetically. Over time, this baked "coalitional aggression" into human psychology.

You can see echoes of this everywhere:

- Young men form gangs, sports teams, or military units where loyalty and fighting spirit are prized.

- War stories often glorify male sacrifice for the tribe, even at great personal cost.

- Rivalries—whether tribal, national, or athletic—still carry the same "band of brothers" flavor.

Altruism, in this sense, is not about kindness for kindness's sake. It's about **tribal survival through cooperation and defense.**

The Nice Tribe Problem

Here's the unsettling part: the better a tribe is at altruism internally, the more dangerous it can be to outsiders. The tighter the bonds of love and loyalty inside the circle, the sharper the hostility at the edges.

Modern example? Think of fiercely bonded sports fans. They'll do anything for each other—buy beers, paint their bodies, scream in solidarity. But when the rival team shows up, that love turns into jeering, insults, sometimes even brawls.

Scale that up to nations, religions, or ethnic groups, and you get war. The very glue that makes groups thrive also makes them clash.

Altruism and violence aren't opposites—they're dance partners. And humans have been dancing this number for tens of thousands of years.

Part II: Fossils, Massacres, and Ancient Rivalries

It's one thing to argue this in theory. It's another thing to look at the evidence carved into the bones of our ancestors. And unfortunately, the archaeological record is clear: prehistoric humans didn't just forage and sing songs. They fought. A lot.

The Fossil Evidence

- **Jebel Sahaba (Sudan, ~13,000 years ago):** Archaeologists found a cemetery with 59 bodies. Nearly half bore signs of violent death—arrowheads embedded in bones, blunt-force trauma to skulls. This wasn't a one-off murder spree; it looked like sustained conflict between groups.

- **Nataruk (Kenya, ~10,000 years ago):** Excavations revealed a massacre site where at least 27 people were killed, including women and children. Some had hands bound. Victims showed skull fractures and arrow wounds. It wasn't raiding for resources—it looked like extermination of a rival group.

- **Crow Creek (South Dakota, ~1325 CE):** A mass grave contained 486 individuals killed in an attack on a fortified village. Evidence suggested torture, mutilation, and burning. This was long before European contact, showing that intergroup violence was already common.

These sites tell a chilling story: organized, group-based violence has been with us since before written history.

Weapons of Friendship and War

The same tools that enabled cooperation—stone axes, bows, spears—were also turned against rivals. Hunting technology doubled as killing technology.

Anthropologists point out that **tool innovation and warfare co-evolved.** Better cooperation meant better weapons, and better weapons meant more intense intergroup conflict.

Think of it as the prehistoric version of the arms race: "They invented sharper spears? Quick, let's invent shields."

Hunter-Gatherers at War

Some like to romanticize hunter-gatherer life as peaceful and egalitarian. And it's true that within groups, cooperation was high. But between groups? Not so much.

Studies of modern hunter-gatherer societies (like the Yanomami in the Amazon, or the Dani of Papua New Guinea) show frequent raiding and warfare. These aren't anomalies—they're windows into the evolutionary past.

Patterns emerge:

- Men form raiding parties.

- Attacks often target men in rival groups (to reduce competition) but can also involve capturing women or resources.

- Success in battle boosts male status and reproductive opportunities.

Again: altruism + aggression, two sides of the same tribal coin.

Why History Keeps Repeating

Fast forward to ancient empires, medieval kingdoms, modern nation-states—it's the same story with better weapons. From the Trojan War to World War II, human history is a loop of tribes (whether clans or countries) loving their own and destroying others.

Even today, the "nice tribe problem" explains why nationalism can slide so easily into xenophobia, or why religious solidarity can morph into holy wars. The deeper the in-group love, the more dangerous the out-group hate.

Everyday Echoes

Before you think this is all doom and gloom, remember: these instincts don't just show up in wars. They echo in everyday life, sometimes comically:

- **Workplace rivalries:** Marketing vs. Sales. Altruism within teams, hostility across departments.

- **Neighborhood disputes:** "Our block throws the best barbecue. Those people across the street? Don't even mow their lawns."

- **Sports fandom:** Manchester United vs. Liverpool. Enough said.

The same psychology that fueled ancient massacres now fuels trash talk and office drama. Which is progress, in its own darkly funny way.

The Big Lesson

Altruism is not unconditionally good. It's conditional: good for *us*, often bad for *them*. The instincts that make humans capable of breathtaking generosity also make us capable of breathtaking cruelty.

This duality is crucial to understand, because it explains why "tribal pride" so often curdles into **collective narcissism.** It's not that humans are evil. It's that our wiring evolved for survival in a hostile world.

The challenge today is figuring out how to keep the best parts of altruism— loyalty, generosity, cooperation—without letting them slide into hostility.

Back to the Campfire

Let's go back to our Stone Age fire. One tribe is laughing, sharing meat, bonding. Across the river, another tribe is doing the same thing. Both are experiencing altruism. Both are feeling love, trust, and unity.

But if those two groups bump into each other tomorrow, the altruism could instantly flip into aggression. Not because they're monsters. But because that's how human survival worked for thousands of years.

This is the **dark side of altruism**: the better we are at loving our own, the easier it is to justify hating others.

Chapter 5: Healthy Pride vs. Fragile Pride

Every family has that one relative who tells the same story over and over again. Maybe it's Uncle Joe and the "touchdown he scored in high school," or Grandma's legendary tale of "the time she met a celebrity in an elevator." The details may or may not line up depending on how much wine has been consumed, but the purpose is always the same: **pride.**

Pride is a double-edged sword. On the one hand, it's motivating, affirming, and community-building. On the other hand, when it tips over into fragility, it becomes exhausting—for the group itself and for everyone around them.

This chapter is about those two faces of pride: the **secure, healthy version** that gives people confidence and cohesion, and the **fragile, defensive version** that spirals into what psychologists call **collective narcissism.**

Healthy Pride: The Good Stuff

Healthy group pride is when people feel a deep sense of satisfaction in their identity or community **without needing constant external validation.**

Think of it like this:

- A kid proudly showing a drawing to their parent.

- A sports fan cheering for their team, win or lose.

- A neighborhood proud of their community garden.

In these cases, pride is rooted in **secure belonging.** It's not about proving superiority or demanding others acknowledge greatness. It's simply enjoying who you are and who you're with.

Psychologists call this **secure group identity.** People with it tend to:

- Feel positive about their group's achievements.

- Cooperate more within the group.

- Show more tolerance toward outsiders (because their pride isn't threatened by difference).

Healthy pride says: *"I'm proud of us."*

Fragile Pride: The Defensive Cousin

Now let's meet healthy pride's neurotic cousin: **fragile pride.**

Fragile pride isn't about feeling good inside. It's about demanding that others recognize your group's greatness—loudly, constantly, and sometimes aggressively.

Fragile pride says: *"I'm proud of us, but if you don't agree, I'll lose my mind."*

This is where **collective narcissism** comes in. Psychologists Agnieszka Golec de Zavala and colleagues have studied this phenomenon in depth. They define it as:

"An emotional investment in an unrealistic belief about the unparalleled greatness of one's group, which requires external validation."

In other words: fragile pride on steroids.

Signs You Might Be in a Narcissistic Group

Collective narcissism has some telltale symptoms:

1. **Hypersensitivity to disrespect.** Any slight, real or imagined, is treated like a personal attack. ("They didn't mention us in the speech? Outrageous!")

2. **Retaliation reflex.** If you're disrespected, you don't just sulk—you lash out.

3. **Constant need for recognition.** "Why doesn't everyone acknowledge how amazing we are?"

4. **Grievance culture.** Dwelling on past slights, refusing to let go.

5. **Fragile self-esteem.** Confidence that cracks under the slightest pressure.

Sound familiar? It should—because this isn't just theory. It's visible in political parties, sports fandoms, religious sects, even friend groups.

Fragile Pride in Action

Let's say two college fraternities, Alpha Squad and Beta Crew, both win trophies. Healthy pride looks like this:

- Alpha Squad: "We're proud of our win. Let's celebrate."

- Beta Crew: "We're proud of our win. Let's celebrate."

Both are satisfied. End of story.

But fragile pride changes the script:

- Alpha Squad: "We're proud of our win. But why didn't the newspaper mention us more? And why is Beta Crew still getting attention? This is a conspiracy!"

- Beta Crew: "They're disrespecting us! Let's retaliate on Twitter!"

Suddenly, what should have been two happy celebrations turns into an arms race of outrage.

The Internet: Fragile Pride's Playground

In the pre-digital age, fragile pride was confined to pubs, parades, and the occasional strongly worded letter to the editor.

Now? Social media has supercharged it.

- Every omission feels like a slight ("Why wasn't my group trending?").
- Every joke feels like mockery.
- Every disagreement feels like betrayal.

On Twitter/X, collective narcissism thrives because the platforms are designed for validation (likes, shares, retweets) and outrage (quote-tweet dunking).

It's no accident that some of the most toxic online communities are also the most fragile. They crave recognition, but any recognition is never enough.

Why Healthy Pride Feels Different

Psychologists have found that **secure group identity** leads to less hostility toward outsiders. Why? Because if you already feel good about your group, you don't need to tear others down to feel validated.

Think of it like secure attachment in relationships:

- A securely attached partner doesn't panic every time their spouse talks to someone else.
- An insecure partner, on the other hand, sees every text message as evidence of betrayal.

Healthy pride is secure attachment at the group level. Fragile pride is jealous, insecure attachment—forever looking for slights, forever needing reassurance.

Nations, Neighborhoods, and Narcissism

Let's scale this up.

- **Healthy national pride:** "I love my country. We've accomplished a lot. I'm proud to be part of it."

- **Fragile national pride:** "My country is the best. Anyone who doesn't admit it is an enemy. If another country does well, they must have cheated."

The same applies at smaller scales:

- **Neighborhoods:** One community might feel proud of their farmers' market (healthy). Another demands constant awards for "Best Town in America" and lashes out if a neighboring town gets recognition (fragile).

- **Religions:** One group quietly practices their faith and finds joy in it (healthy). Another insists theirs is the only "true" faith and feels persecuted by Starbucks cups (fragile).

Humor Break: Signs Your Group Has Fragile Pride

- You spend more time complaining about "lack of respect" than actually doing things worth respecting.

- Half your group meetings are about conspiracy theories of how "they" are holding you down.

- Your group motto might as well be: "We're special, why won't everyone admit it?!"

- Outsiders don't even know there's a conflict, but you're already planning revenge.

Why Fragile Pride Turns Dangerous

Fragile pride isn't just annoying—it's dangerous. Because once you define your group's worth by external validation, you're at the mercy of outsiders' opinions. And outsiders will *never* validate you enough.

That constant dissatisfaction fuels aggression:

- "They're ignoring us" → resentment.

- "They're disrespecting us" → retaliation.

- "They're conspiring against us" → paranoia and violence.

Fragile pride is like being perpetually hangry. You're never full, and you're always one slight away from snapping.

The Link to Collective Narcissism

Here's the key connection: fragile pride is the **emotional fuel** of collective narcissism.

Collective narcissism takes the insecurity of fragile pride and builds a full worldview around it:

- "We are great, but nobody recognizes it."

- "We are victims of unfair treatment."

- "We must fight until we get the respect we deserve."

And once enough people in a group buy into this narrative, the result is political polarization, intergroup hostility, or even war.

The Big Lesson

Pride, like fire, is neutral. It can warm your house or burn it down.

- **Healthy pride** strengthens groups without attacking others. It's secure, confident, and open.

- **Fragile pride** creates insecurity, paranoia, and aggression. It demands constant recognition and lashes out when it doesn't get it.

Understanding this difference is the first step to recognizing when your group is slipping from healthy pride into narcissism. Because once you're in narcissism territory, the path ahead gets rocky fast.

Back to the Family Dinner

So, let's go back to Uncle Joe and his high school touchdown story. If he tells it with a smile, enjoying the memory without needing everyone else to bow down, that's healthy pride.

But if he gets angry when no one claps, accuses the family of disrespect, and storms out declaring that "this family never supports me," that's fragile pride.

Multiply Uncle Joe by a million, and you've got collective narcissism.

The rest of this book is about what happens when fragile pride scales up—when entire nations, religions, or political movements become Uncle Joe at the dinner table, demanding applause and picking fights when they don't get it.

Chapter 6: Collective Narcissism Unmasked (Part I & II)

Part I: The Fragile Core

When we hear the word "narcissism," we usually think of that one guy at the office who talks about his CrossFit routine until you consider faking a Wi-Fi outage just to escape. But narcissism isn't just about individuals. Whole groups can act like narcissists—self-important, insecure, hypersensitive, and perpetually outraged.

That's **collective narcissism.**

Unlike healthy group pride, which is confident and secure, collective narcissism is fragile. It's the psychological equivalent of a balloon: shiny on the outside, but one tiny pinprick of criticism and—*pop!*

So what does a narcissistic group look like? Let's break down the profile.

Symptom #1: Hypersensitivity to Disrespect

Collective narcissists walk around with their radar tuned to "insult detection." If their group isn't constantly praised, they interpret it as an attack.

- **A country** not mentioned in an international speech? Proof of disrespect.

- **A fan base** not acknowledged in an award speech? Outrage.

- **A political party** left out of a poll? Conspiracy.

It's not enough for the group to succeed—they also need everyone else to publicly recognize their greatness. Otherwise, they feel wounded.

Psychologists call this **hostile attribution bias**: assuming malice where there may be none. It's the same impulse that makes your paranoid friend think the waiter "hates them" because he forgot the extra ranch dressing.

Symptom #2: Retaliation Reflex

Once disrespected—real or imagined—collective narcissists don't shrug it off. They retaliate.

This retaliation can take many forms:

- Political groups launching smear campaigns.

- Fan bases flooding comment sections.

- Nations escalating diplomatic insults into international crises.

The logic goes like this: "If they disrespect us, we must strike back to restore honor." It's a vicious cycle, because each retaliation triggers another perceived slight, which demands more retaliation.

At scale, this is how flame wars, culture wars, and even literal wars get fueled.

Symptom #3: Grievance Culture

Collective narcissism thrives on grievances. These groups keep long mental ledgers of every slight, injustice, or insult.

It's like they're carrying around a scrapbook titled *"Everyone Who Ever Wronged Us"*—complete with receipts, footnotes, and dramatic flair.

Even past wounds that have healed elsewhere remain raw in narcissistic groups. They define themselves by what was *done to them* rather than by what they *do*.

This creates an endless cycle of resentment. Instead of moving forward, the group stays stuck in an emotional time machine, replaying old betrayals to justify new hostility.

Symptom #4: Fragile Self-Esteem

Ironically, for all their chest-thumping, collective narcissists don't actually feel secure. Their pride is brittle.

- They need outsiders to constantly affirm their greatness.

- They interpret silence as disrespect.

- They collapse under criticism, even mild or constructive.

This fragility makes them both exhausting and dangerous. Imagine trying to date someone who bursts into tears because you didn't like their Instagram post. Now multiply that by a million people, and you've got a narcissistic movement.

Part II: The Toxic Consequences

So far, we've seen the fragile emotional core of collective narcissism. But what happens when you put those traits into motion? The result isn't just insecurity—it's toxic behavior with real-world consequences.

Consequence #1: Conspiracy Thinking

When collective narcissists feel disrespected, they often leap to conspiracy theories. After all, if "we" are so obviously great, then the only explanation for not being recognized is that "they" are plotting against us.

This leads to elaborate theories about hidden enemies, unfair systems, or secret cabals. The conspiracy lens explains everything:

- "The media is deliberately ignoring us."

- "Other nations are undermining us."

- "The system is rigged to keep us down."

Conspiracies serve a psychological purpose: they allow groups to externalize failure. Instead of facing their own shortcomings, they can blame "the plot."

Consequence #2: Generalized Prejudice

Collective narcissism doesn't just stop at one out-group. It often spreads like a contagion into prejudice against *many* out-groups.

Why? Because once you start seeing outsiders as "disrespectful," it's easy to lump them all together. "They" become a faceless mass of enemies, even if the groups are unrelated.

This is why collective narcissism often fuels xenophobia, racism, or religious intolerance. It's not about specific grievances anymore—it's about defining outsiders in general as dangerous and unworthy.

Consequence #3: Betrayal from Within

Here's the ironic twist: narcissistic groups often end up harming themselves.

Because collective narcissists are so fragile and so obsessed with status, they're prone to internal rivalries and betrayals.

- Leaders hoard recognition and punish dissent.

- Members turn on each other for not being "loyal enough."

- The group fractures into sub-groups, each accusing the others of betrayal.

In the end, the narcissistic drive for validation corrodes the very group it was meant to protect.

Case Studies in Collective Narcissism

Let's ground this in some recognizable examples (without naming names too directly, since, well… collective narcissists don't like being called out).

- **Politics:** Political parties that frame themselves as "the only true patriots," interpreting any criticism as treason.

- **Nationalism:** Countries that constantly claim to be "unfairly treated" on the world stage, regardless of evidence.

- **Fandoms:** Music or movie fan bases that attack anyone who gives less than five stars to their idol's latest work.

- **Workplaces:** Departments that obsess over recognition, accusing management of bias whenever another team gets praised.

Different scales, same psychology: fragile pride, grievance, retaliation.

Humor Break: If Your Group Were a Person…

If collective narcissism were an individual, they'd be that friend who:

- Constantly talks about how underappreciated they are.

- Sees every minor inconvenience as a personal attack.

- Needs endless reassurance but snaps at you if you don't give it.

- Secretly stalks their ex on social media and mutters about conspiracies.

Now imagine trying to build a country—or a global society—out of *millions* of that person. Exactly.

Why Collective Narcissism Matters

This isn't just about theory. Collective narcissism explains some of the most pressing issues of our time:

- Why political polarization feels so toxic.

- Why conspiracy theories spread like wildfire.

- Why groups that should be united often end up fracturing.

At its heart, collective narcissism is a mismatch between **ancient tribal instincts** and **modern global society.** Our brains crave validation for our small tribes, but our world is too big, too interconnected, and too diverse for that craving to ever be satisfied.

The Big Lesson

Healthy pride says: *"We're proud of who we are."*

Collective narcissism says: *"We're proud of who we are—unless you don't recognize it, in which case we'll destroy you."*

One builds community. The other builds conflict.

And here's the kicker: the line between the two is thin. Groups can slide from healthy pride into narcissism without even noticing. That's why it's so important to learn the warning signs—before we find ourselves in a full-blown grievance spiral.

Back to Uncle Joe (Again)

Remember Uncle Joe and his high school touchdown story? In Chapter 5, he was just fragile. But now, imagine he gathers other relatives, forms a coalition, and starts demanding the entire family acknowledge his touchdown as "the greatest moment in family history."

He insists the local newspaper deliberately ignored him. He lashes out at cousins who don't clap loudly enough. He accuses Grandma of secretly siding with "the enemy."

That's no longer just Uncle Joe being annoying. That's Uncle Joe leading a collective narcissistic movement. And if Thanksgiving isn't careful, it's about to end in a food fight.

Interlude #2: A Narcissistic Group Walks Into a Bar...

It's a quiet evening at O'Malley's Pub when the door bursts open and in marches a group called **The League of Unfairly Underappreciated People (LUUP)**. They've just come from a rally where they demanded recognition for being "the most special group in history," but now they need beers—and validation.

The Arrival

The bartender, used to rowdy crowds, asks cheerfully, "What'll it be?"

The LUUP members exchange shocked looks.

"What'll it be?" their leader hisses. "What'll it BE?! Don't you know who we ARE?"

"Uh... customers?" the bartender guesses.

"Wrong!" says the leader. "We are the *most important customers you will ever serve.* And if you don't acknowledge that, it's an insult to our dignity."

The bartender blinks. "Okay, well... do you want pints or bottles?"

"Pints," the leader declares. "But only if you pour them with proper respect."

The Slights Begin

As the pints arrive, one member notices the glasses aren't frosted. Outrage erupts.

"They gave us warm glasses because they don't respect us!"

51

Another member points to a group at a nearby table. "Did you hear them whisper? They're mocking us! They're probably plotting to steal our fries."

A third member slams their pint on the table. "And why is THEIR table closer to the dartboard? This is discrimination!"

Within minutes, the LUUP members are convinced the entire bar is conspiring against them.

Retaliation Reflex

The group springs into action.

- They demand the bartender apologize—publicly, in front of all patrons.

- They insist the dartboard table be reassigned to them.

- They loudly recount a list of every bar that's "disrespected" them in the past.

When one regular dares to say, "Hey, chill out—it's just a bar," the LUUP members gasp in unison.

"Did you hear that? He wants to erase us!"

Conspiracy Time

By round two, the LUUP members have developed a full conspiracy theory: the bartender, the dart players, and even the jukebox are in league against them.

"The jukebox didn't play our song request," one insists. "Proof of systemic bias!"

Another whispers, "The dartboard is rigged. They don't want us to win."

Soon, the entire bar is divided: half rolling their eyes, the other half avoiding eye contact in case they're accused of disrespect.

The Implosion

Eventually, the LUUP turns on itself. One member accuses another of not being "outraged enough."

"You didn't slam your pint down as hard as the rest of us. Are you even loyal?"

Infighting erupts. Half the group storms out, declaring the others "traitors." The remaining members stay behind, sulking and demanding the bartender offer them free nachos as reparations.

The Moral of the Story

By closing time, O'Malley's is exhausted. The bartender sighs and mutters:

"Never again. Next time, I'd rather host a bachelorette party with karaoke."

The moral? Collective narcissism doesn't just make groups fragile—it makes them unbearable drinking companions. They demand endless recognition, see insults everywhere, retaliate at the drop of a hat, spin conspiracy theories, and eventually fracture from their own internal drama.

It's funny in a bar. It's dangerous in politics, nations, or global conflicts.

Chapter 7: Modern Accelerants (Part I & II)

Part I: Politics as the New Tribal Religion

Back in the Stone Age, tribes bonded through rituals, myths, and shared hunts. In medieval times, it was religion—cathedrals, hymns, holy days—that bound communities. Today? For many, politics has taken over that role.

That might sound cynical, but the parallels are striking.

Faith and Factions

- **Rituals:** Instead of Sunday services, we now have campaign rallies and conventions. Instead of incense and hymns, we wave banners and chant slogans.

- **Sacred texts:** Party platforms, founding documents, and key speeches are studied and quoted like scripture.

- **Saints and devils:** Leaders are idolized as saviors or demonized as villains.

Like religion, politics now serves as a source of **identity** as much as belief. People don't just say, "I voted for this policy." They say, "I *am* this kind of person."

Identity Fusion

Psychologists call this **identity fusion**: when your personal identity fuses with your group identity. In this state, an attack on the group feels like an attack on *you personally*.

This explains why political debates so often feel toxic. It's not just disagreement about policy—it's a perceived assault on who people are.

In experiments, people with fused political identities are more willing to make personal sacrifices—even violence—for their group. That's tribal loyalty dialed up to eleven.

The Death of Cross-Cutting Ties

In the past, people belonged to multiple overlapping communities. You might be a steelworker, a union member, a churchgoer, a bowling league captain, and a Democrat. Or a farmer, a church deacon, a veteran, and a Republican.

Those cross-cutting ties meant your identity wasn't just one thing. If politics got tense, you still shared beers with the other side at the bowling alley.

But in recent decades, those overlapping identities have weakened. Church attendance has dropped, unions have declined, and local clubs have faded. Politics has moved into the vacuum.

Now, for many, politics isn't one identity among many—it's the *primary* identity. And that makes us hyper-tribal.

News as the Pulpit

Add media into the mix. In polarized societies, people don't just consume news—they consume **identity-affirming sermons.**

Cable channels, talk radio, partisan websites—they don't just inform. They reassure the tribe that it's right and the outsiders are wrong. News becomes a loyalty ritual: "Our tribe's truth vs. their lies."

It's no wonder political opponents increasingly see each other not as rivals, but as enemies. This is politics as religion, and every election feels like holy war.

Part II: The Algorithmic Village Bonfire

If politics is the new religion, then social media is the megachurch and the bonfire combined—complete with smoke machines, shouting, and the occasional brawl in the parking lot.

The problem? Social media is designed not for truth, but for engagement. And what engages us most? Outrage, tribalism, and narcissism.

Outrage as Currency

Platforms like Twitter/X, Facebook, TikTok, and YouTube run on algorithms that maximize time spent scrolling. What keeps people scrolling? Content that triggers strong emotions—especially anger.

- A cute puppy video will get a smile.
- A political insult will get a click, a share, and a furious all-nighter.

This is how social media becomes an **outrage amplifier.** Groups already primed for grievance find endless fuel.

Echo Chambers and Rabbit Holes

Social media also sorts people into **echo chambers.** Algorithms learn your preferences and serve you more of the same. If you click on one conspiracy theory, you'll soon be served ten more.

This isn't unique to politics: if you watch one sourdough tutorial, YouTube assumes you're starting a bakery. But when applied to tribal identity, the result is dangerous. People spiral deeper into their in-group worldview, seeing only validation and never challenge.

Over time, the echo chamber doesn't just reinforce beliefs—it radicalizes them.

Global Insecurity, Local Rage

Social media also magnifies a peculiar mismatch: global insecurity translated into local tribal rage.

- A farmer in Nebraska or a shopkeeper in Poland may feel distant global economic forces shaking their lives.

- Instead of understanding complex global systems, their brains default to the simpler, older framework: "We are being disrespected by *them*."

And online communities gladly supply scapegoats. Suddenly, complex global anxiety becomes targeted grievance at outsiders—immigrants, elites, foreign powers, rival groups.

Case Study: The Viral Outrage Cycle

Here's how it works, step by step:

1. Someone posts a minor slight against a group.

2. The post goes viral in echo chambers.

3. Group members interpret it as evidence of systemic disrespect.

4. They retaliate online (hashtags, insults, pile-ons).

5. Outsiders see the overreaction and mock it.

6. The group interprets the mockery as *further proof* of disrespect.

It's a self-fueling cycle. Outrage produces more outrage until everyone's burnt out—but the algorithms are delighted.

Everyday Tribal Firestorms

It's easy to laugh at viral outrage, but it follows the same psychology as Stone Age tribal defense:

- **Tribe A:** "They disrespected us!"

- **Tribe B:** "Their overreaction proves they're ridiculous!"

- **Tribe A:** "See?! They're mocking us again! Attack!"

Instead of spears and arrows, it's hashtags and memes. But the tribal brain doesn't know the difference.

The Feedback Loop of Fragility

Social media doesn't just amplify collective narcissism—it rewards it. Groups that shout the loudest about disrespect gain attention, clicks, and followers. Outrage becomes currency.

The result? Fragile pride isn't corrected—it's validated and monetized. The digital bonfire burns hotter.

The Big Lesson

Politics fused with identity + algorithms that amplify outrage = the perfect storm for collective narcissism.

- Politics has become the new tribal religion, leaving little room for compromise.

- Social media turns grievances into global bonfires, rewarding fragility instead of resilience.

- Our Stone Age brains, wired for 150-person tribes, are being hijacked by billion-person platforms.

The accelerants are modern, but the fire is ancient.

Back to the Pub

Remember our LUUP friends (The League of Unfairly Underappreciated People) from the last interlude? Imagine what happens when they get smartphones.

- They start live-tweeting the bartender's "insult."

- Their outrage trends under #RespectLUUP.

- A rival bar across town mocks them with memes.

- LUUP members escalate, posting conspiracy threads about a "Bar Cabal."

By morning, nobody remembers who poured the beer, but thousands of strangers have joined the fight.

That's the world we live in: local slights, global bonfires, endless outrage.

Chapter 8: Empathy — Humanity's Superpower (Part I & II)

Part I: Emotional Wi-Fi — The Neuroscience of Empathy

Imagine you're watching someone stub their toe. You wince, clutch your own foot, and mutter "ouch!" even though your toes are perfectly fine. That's empathy in action. Your brain just borrowed their pain signal and ran it through your own system.

Empathy is often described as "walking in someone else's shoes," but neuroscientists might call it **"running someone else's code."** It's one of humanity's most extraordinary tricks: the ability to resonate with another person's experience so deeply that it feels like your own.

Mirror Neurons: The Brain's Copycat Circuit

Back in the 1990s, researchers in Parma, Italy, discovered something astonishing while studying monkeys. When the monkeys watched researchers grab peanuts, the same neurons fired as when the monkeys grabbed peanuts themselves.

These cells were dubbed **mirror neurons.** Their job? To "mirror" the actions and emotions of others.

Humans have these too. When you see someone smile, neurons in your brain's motor system fire as if you were smiling. When you see someone cry, your emotional circuits light up as though you're on the verge of tears.

It's emotional Wi-Fi: you pick up the signal automatically.

The Pain Circuit

Empathy isn't just about actions—it's about feelings. Neuroscientists have found that when you see someone in pain, areas of your brain like the anterior insula and anterior cingulate cortex light up—the same areas that process *your own pain.*

This is why you can't watch cringe videos without cringing. Your brain is wired to co-experience. It doesn't politely observe; it joins in.

Emotional Contagion

Ever notice how laughter spreads in a room, or how yawns are contagious? That's empathy at work. Emotional states leap from person to person like viruses.

- A joyful coworker lifts the office mood.

- A grumpy boss infects everyone's afternoon.

- A friend's panic makes you panic too.

We don't just influence each other's emotions—we *share* them. We are, in a very real sense, Wi-Fi routers of feelings.

Why Empathy Was a Survival Tool

All of this isn't just touchy-feely sentiment. Empathy was essential for survival.

- Mothers needed to read babies' cries instinctively.

- Hunters had to coordinate without endless explanation.

- Tribes needed to sense trust, fear, or joy in each other instantly.

Groups with stronger empathy bonds cooperated better, stuck together, and survived.

That's why empathy feels so natural. It's not a luxury—it's an ancient survival feature.

Part II: Why Empathy Works Best for "Us"

Here's the twist: empathy isn't universal. It's selective. It evolved to work best for people inside your circle—the ones your survival depended on.

That's why we can feel a stranger's stubbed toe on TikTok, but sometimes shrug at massive tragedies far away. Our empathy has a radius.

The Empathy Bias

Studies show that people consistently feel more empathy for:

- Those who look like them.

- Those in their in-group (same team, nationality, political party).

- Those they can identify with personally.

Meanwhile, empathy often plummets for:

- Outsiders.

- Rivals.

- People we've been taught to see as "them."

This isn't because we're heartless. It's because our brains evolved in small tribes where caring about outsiders was inefficient—or even dangerous.

The Brain Scan Proof

In experiments where participants watch both in-group and out-group members experience pain, their brains literally light up differently.

- In-group suffering activates empathy circuits.

- Out-group suffering? Much weaker response—or in some cases, even activation of reward circuits. (Yes: people sometimes take pleasure in the pain of rivals.)

That's empathy's dark limitation: it's not evenly distributed. It's biased.

Stadium Empathy

You've seen this play out in sports. A player on your team twists an ankle—you wince, groan, maybe even tear up.

A player on the rival team twists an ankle—you might smirk or think, "Well, that helps us." The same injury, but your empathy is filtered by tribal identity.

It's the empathy gap in its purest (and pettiest) form.

Why Global Empathy Feels Overwhelming

In a world of eight billion people, this selective empathy becomes a problem. Our brains weren't built to process the suffering of strangers on the other side of the planet.

When we're bombarded with global crises, our empathy circuits get overloaded. We either shut down (compassion fatigue) or retreat to our small circles where empathy feels manageable.

That's why one news story about a single rescued puppy can get more emotional response than statistics about thousands of displaced families. The puppy feels like "us." The statistics feel like "them."

The Empathy Mismatch

So empathy is both our superpower and our Achilles' heel. It makes human connection possible, but it also creates bias, exclusion, and indifference.

It explains:

- Why communities can be deeply compassionate internally while being cruel externally.

- Why tragedies at home feel unbearable, but tragedies abroad feel abstract.

- Why political tribes can't bridge divides—they're literally feeling different levels of empathy for their own versus their rivals.

The Big Lesson

Empathy is humanity's greatest strength—but it's also selective, fragile, and biased. It was designed for Stone Age villages, not global societies.

If we want to harness it for modern challenges, we need to understand its wiring:

- **Mirror neurons** make us share feelings automatically.

- **Tribal bias** makes us share selectively.

- **Out-group gaps** create blind spots that fuel prejudice and conflict.

We don't need to throw out empathy. We need to upgrade it.

Back to the Campfire

Imagine two tribes around their separate fires. Each is laughing, sharing food, bonding through empathy. Their brains are humming with connection.

But if those tribes bump into each other the next morning, empathy might switch off instantly. The laughter, the warmth, the shared humanity—it stops at the boundary of "us."

That's empathy's paradox: it unites us inside the circle but abandons us at the edge.

The next chapters will explore what happens at those edges—why we cry for puppies but not for strangers, why we sometimes cheer at rivals' pain, and whether it's possible to stretch the circle wider.

Because if empathy is our superpower, the question is: can we learn to use it for *everyone*—or will we keep saving it for our own tribe?

Chapter 9: The Empathy Gap — Why We Cry for Puppies but Not for Strangers

Picture this: you're scrolling through social media when a heartbreaking video pops up. A tiny puppy has been rescued from a storm drain. It's wet, shivering, and squeaking pathetically. You tear up. You send the video to your friend. You consider donating to the animal shelter.

Five minutes later, you scroll past a headline: *"Thousands Displaced by Flooding in Southeast Asia."* You sigh, maybe click "sad face" if you're feeling generous, and keep scrolling to check your notifications.

Welcome to the empathy gap: the strange, sometimes cruel mismatch between the feelings we extend to those inside our circle and the relative indifference we show toward those outside it.

Why Puppies Win

Let's start with the obvious: puppies are emotional cheat codes. They're small, helpless, and biologically engineered to trigger our caregiving instincts (those big eyes, floppy ears, and squeaks mimic infant cues). Our Stone Age brains respond instantly: *Protect! Care! Feed!*

But humans? Strangers halfway around the world? That's trickier. Our empathy wasn't built for statistics or headlines. It was built for faces, voices, and direct contact. We evolved in tribes where everyone's suffering was personal and visible.

When empathy circuits encounter abstraction—numbers, distant places, people we can't imagine—they sputter. The puppy gets tears. The flood victims get a skim.

The Psychology of the Empathy Gap

Psychologists and neuroscientists have spent decades trying to understand why our empathy is so uneven. Here are some of the biggest culprits:

1. The Identifiable Victim Effect

We're far more likely to empathize with *one person we can picture* than with thousands we can't.

- A single photo of a malnourished child inspires more donations than statistics about millions at risk.

- One dramatic rescue gets global attention while chronic suffering gets ignored.

Paul Slovic, a psychologist who studies compassion, famously summed it up: *"The more who die, the less we care."*

It's not that we're cruel—it's that our brains struggle to scale empathy beyond the individual.

2. In-Group Bias

As we saw in Chapter 8, empathy is biased toward people who feel like "us." We identify more strongly with those who share our language, culture, appearance, or values.

- Americans feel a bigger emotional punch from a U.S. hurricane than an identical one abroad.

- Fans empathize more with an injured player on their own team than the rival's star.

- People often donate more to local causes, even if global needs are greater.

Our empathy map has boundaries, and it lights up brightest at home.

3. Compassion Fatigue

Empathy is like a muscle: powerful, but exhaustible. When bombarded with tragedy after tragedy, we start to shut down.

- The first news of a disaster gets a flood of donations. The third or fourth gets shrugs.

- Aid workers and doctors often burn out because constant exposure to suffering overwhelms their circuits.

We want to care, but our brains can't sustain high empathy indefinitely.

4. Out-Group Dehumanization

Sometimes, it's not just that we care less. Sometimes, we actively **turn off empathy** for outsiders.

In brain scan studies, people showed strong empathy for in-group members in pain, but far weaker responses for out-group members. In some cases, they even showed activity in reward circuits—meaning they felt pleasure at rivals' suffering.

Yes, you read that right: empathy isn't just biased; it sometimes flips into its evil twin.

Schadenfreude and Glückschmerz

Let's pause for two delightful German words that describe this darker side of empathy:

- **Schadenfreude**: joy at someone else's misfortune. (Like when your annoying coworker's big presentation goes horribly wrong and you secretly feel giddy.)

- **Glückschmerz**: pain at someone else's good fortune. (Like when your ex posts vacation pics with their new partner and you feel sick, even though you're "totally over them.")

These emotions may sound petty, but they're tribal instincts. We instinctively root for rivals to fail, because in a zero-sum world, their loss feels like our gain.

Sports: A Safe Laboratory for Tribal Schadenfreude

Sports fandom is one of the clearest modern windows into empathy's biases.

- When a rival player gets injured, some fans cheer.

- When your team wins, their joy feels like your joy. When they lose, their pain feels like your pain.

- Rival victories feel like personal defeats.

No wonder stadiums sometimes look less like entertainment venues and more like Stone Age war camps with better snacks.

The Global Empathy Crisis

The empathy gap isn't just about puppies and sports. It has profound consequences for global issues.

- **Humanitarian crises:** People donate generously after dramatic events (like tsunamis) but often ignore chronic issues (like famine).

- **Climate change:** Future generations feel abstract. Polar bears get more sympathy than people in developing nations already suffering.

- **Refugees and migrants:** Empathy is often blocked by stereotypes and "out-group" framing.

Our tribal empathy circuits were perfect for village life, but they short-circuit when faced with global interdependence.

Humor Break: Everyday Empathy Gaps

To bring it down to the everyday level, consider these scenarios:

- You cry at a dog-food commercial featuring sad-eyed shelter pets, but when your neighbor tells you about their third divorce, you just nod and say, "Yikes."

- You feel bad for a fictional character on Netflix but mute the news about real suffering.

- You donate to save koalas in Australia but not to help the family across town who needs a new roof.

This doesn't make you a monster—it makes you human. But it also highlights the mismatch between our ancient brains and our modern moral responsibilities.

Can We Expand the Circle?

The good news: empathy isn't fixed. It's flexible. We can push the boundaries outward if we know the tricks.

Psychologists have studied ways to "hack" the empathy gap:

- **Humanize statistics:** Pair numbers with stories of real individuals.

- **Increase contact:** Meeting and interacting with outsiders can boost empathy.

- **Reframe identity:** Expanding "us" to include broader groups ("we're all parents," "we're all citizens of Earth").

- **Art and storytelling:** Novels, films, and media can make outsiders feel like insiders.

None of this is easy. But it shows that empathy, while biased, isn't unchangeable.

The Big Lesson

Empathy is powerful, but it's not fair. It's selective, biased, and easily overloaded. That's why we cry for puppies and shrug at statistics, cheer when rivals fail, and sometimes ignore strangers in need.

But recognizing the gap is the first step to bridging it. Once we understand how empathy works—and fails—we can start designing societies, media, and institutions that stretch our caring muscles further than nature intended.

Back to the Coffee Shop

Remember the neon-shirted tourists from Chapter 3? Your brain instantly filed them as "not us." But imagine if you sat with them, shared a laugh, heard their stories. Suddenly, your empathy circuits might switch on. They'd go from faceless outsiders to part of your circle.

That's the hope. That empathy can stretch—not effortlessly, not infinitely, but deliberately.

The real question is: can we scale it fast enough to meet the challenges of a global, interconnected world? Or will we keep crying for puppies while ignoring the flood victims scrolling past on our screens?

Interlude #3: How to Hack Empathy — Sort Of

If empathy is humanity's superpower, it sometimes feels like one of those gadgets you bought off late-night TV: impressive in theory, unpredictable in practice, and prone to breaking at the worst times.

The truth is, empathy doesn't come with a universal on/off switch. It's messy, biased, and selective. But that doesn't mean we're stuck with our default settings. With a little creativity (and a lot of humility), we can *hack* empathy—kind of.

Here are some semi-serious, semi-silly "hacks" to stretch your empathy muscles beyond their Stone Age defaults.

Hack #1: Pretend Everyone's in Your Tribe

Your brain is wired to care about "us" and ignore "them." So the trick? Expand your definition of "us."

- That guy cutting you off in traffic? Imagine he's your cousin, late for the same family barbecue.

- The barista who got your order wrong? Pretend she's your niece learning her first job.

- The rival sports fan screaming insults? Think of him as your loud uncle who can't control his volume.

Will it make them less annoying? Not necessarily. But it'll trigger the "in-group" circuits that make your brain soften its stance.

Hack #2: Use Netflix as Empathy Training

Stories are empathy steroids. When you binge a series, you start caring about fictional people as if they're your neighbors.

So why not use this power for good? Watch shows, movies, or documentaries that feature people wildly different from you. Your brain doesn't care if it's scripted—the emotional Wi-Fi still works.

Just be careful. This is how you end up weeping over a cartoon fish while ignoring texts from your actual friends.

Hack #3: Find Common Ground (Yes, Even Pizza)

Nothing unites rivals like discovering they share a taste for pepperoni.

Shared identities—parenthood, hobbies, even food preferences—can override tribal divides. That's why peace negotiators sometimes start with meals. It's harder to demonize someone once you've both spilled tomato sauce on your shirts.

So next time you're locked in a political argument, try asking: "But do you like pineapple on pizza?" If the answer is yes, congratulations—you've just built a fragile but real bridge.

Hack #4: Flip the Script

Instead of asking, *"Why are they like that?"* try asking, *"When have I been like that?"*

This reframe turns judgment into empathy. For example:

- The "lazy coworker" → remember the time you phoned it in on a project.

- The "rude stranger" → recall when you snapped at someone on a bad day.

- The "selfish friend" → think of the times you put yourself first, too.

It doesn't excuse behavior, but it helps you see the shared humanity.

Hack #5: Practice Micro-Empathies

Big global crises can overwhelm your circuits. But empathy doesn't have to be grand—it can be practiced in tiny daily doses.

- Make eye contact with the cashier and actually mean your "thank you."

- Ask your coworker how their weekend was and *listen to the answer.*

- Send a "just thinking of you" text to someone in your outer circle.

Small acts keep the empathy muscles toned without burning you out.

Hack #6: Embrace the Absurd

Sometimes empathy works best when we lighten up. Humor can sneak past defenses where lectures fail.

Imagine if, instead of UN summits with long speeches, world leaders had to spend the first 15 minutes complimenting each other's pets. Or trade embarrassing stories. Or sing karaoke.

Ridiculous? Absolutely. But it's hard to declare war on someone after you've both botched *"Bohemian Rhapsody"* together.

The Fine Print

Now, a word of caution. These hacks aren't magic. They don't erase centuries of tribal wiring or guarantee world peace. Your rival fan may still heckle you. The barista may still misspell your name. Pineapple on pizza may still divide households.

Empathy is stubborn, and hacking it takes practice. Sometimes it works beautifully. Sometimes it fails hilariously. But even when it fails, it leaves you with a story—and maybe a laugh.

The Big Idea

The point isn't to become an empathy superhero overnight. It's to stretch the circle, just a little. To remind yourself that "them" and "us" aren't as fixed as your brain insists.

Every time you trick your mind into treating someone as part of your tribe— even briefly—you chip away at the empathy gap. And in a world running on outrage, those small hacks add up.

Chapter 10: When Empathy Backfires
(Part I & II)

Part I: Perspective-Taking Gone Wrong

We've spent the last two chapters praising empathy as humanity's superpower. And it is! But like all superpowers, it comes with a dark side.

Think of Spider-Man: he can swing across cities, but he also accidentally smashes through Aunt May's window. Empathy is the same—it can heal or it can hurt, depending on how it's used.

The Trouble with Perspective-Taking

One of the classic empathy strategies is **perspective-taking**: imagining what life is like in someone else's shoes. Sounds noble, right?

But here's the problem: humans are *terrible* at imagining life in shoes they've never worn.

- When members of one group try to imagine the experiences of another, they often project their own biases.

- Sometimes, they overestimate how hard things are ("Your life must be unbearable!").

- Other times, they underestimate ("It can't be that bad. I'd handle it fine.").

In both cases, empathy doesn't bridge the gap—it reinforces stereotypes.

Metastereotypes: "What They Think We Think They Think"

Here's where it gets extra messy.

When you try to take someone else's perspective, you don't just imagine their feelings—you also imagine what *they* think *you* think about them. These are called **metastereotypes**, and they're like empathy funhouse mirrors.

Example:

- Group A imagines how Group B feels.

- But while doing that, Group A also thinks: "They probably think we see them as lazy."

- So Group A says something overly sympathetic like, "I know it must be hard, with all the disadvantages you face…"

- Group B bristles: "Wow, you really *do* think we're lazy."

Congratulations: empathy just backfired.

The Awkward Workshop

Picture a corporate diversity training where employees are told to "imagine life as someone from another background."

- One employee awkwardly role-plays as an immigrant, exaggerating accents.

- Another imagines being poor, but can't resist commenting, "I'd just budget better."

- Everyone leaves feeling worse, not better.

That's empathy gone wrong—not because people didn't try, but because imagining another's experience is harder than it looks.

Empathy Fatigue as a Backfire

Even when empathy is accurate, it can overwhelm.

Doctors, nurses, social workers—people in high-empathy jobs—often burn out. They feel others' pain so deeply that they become emotionally exhausted. The result? Numbness. Detachment. Sometimes even hostility as a defensive shield.

This isn't a failure of character—it's empathy overshooting its mark.

Part II: Expanding the Circle — With a Few Explosions

So if direct perspective-taking is unreliable, what about strategies to *expand empathy* to outsiders? Great idea in theory. But in practice? It can backfire too.

Recategorization: The Double-Edged Sword

Psychologists often talk about **recategorization**—shifting people from "them" into "us."

For example: Instead of "immigrants" vs. "natives," reframe as "workers" or "parents." Instead of "rival fans," reframe as "sports lovers."

When it works, it's beautiful. People find common ground, empathy expands, bridges form.

But when it fails, it fails loudly. If people reject the new category, they may become even *more* entrenched in hostility.

Example:

- A campaign says, "We're all global citizens."

- Some people respond: "No, we're not. Stop trying to erase my identity!"

- Result: more polarization, not less.

Contact Gone Wrong

Another classic empathy intervention is **contact theory**: get groups together under structured conditions, and prejudice will decrease.

But not all contact works. When it's forced or poorly designed, it can worsen tensions.

Imagine a school program that forces rival groups to sit together and share lunch. Instead of bonding, the kids spend the whole time glaring at each other, muttering insults, and leaving with fresh grievances.

The lesson: empathy needs the right conditions. Otherwise, it curdles.

When Rivalries Intensify

Sometimes, attempts to humanize rivals can make hostility spike.

- Fans who watch documentaries about rival teams sometimes end up hating them more ("Wow, they're not just arrogant—they're *systematically* arrogant!").

- Politically, hearing the "personal stories" of opponents can backfire if people interpret them as manipulative or self-pitying.

Instead of creating empathy, the exercise entrenches contempt.

The Limits of Emotional Wi-Fi

The real problem is that empathy isn't a neutral tool—it's filtered through tribal identity.

- If someone is in your in-group, empathy deepens connection.

- If someone is in your out-group, empathy attempts can feel like pity, condescension, or manipulation.

Our brains didn't evolve for "universal empathy." They evolved for **tribal empathy.** Trying to stretch it too far, too fast, sometimes makes the elastic snap.

Humor Break: Everyday Empathy Failures

- You tell a friend, "I know exactly how you feel," after they've lost a parent—because you once lost your cat. They don't laugh.

- Your coworker vents about job stress. You say, "I get it. That's why I meditate for two hours every morning." They glare.

- A politician says, "I feel your pain," while wearing a $10,000 suit. The crowd boos.

Sometimes, trying too hard to empathize just highlights the gap.

The Big Lesson

Empathy is powerful—but it's not always reliable. It can:

- Reinforce stereotypes instead of breaking them.

- Overwhelm caregivers until they shut down.

- Backfire when recategorization feels forced.

- Deepen divides when pity replaces respect.

The trick isn't to abandon empathy. It's to wield it wisely. To recognize when it helps, when it harms, and when it needs structure to work.

Back to the Campfire

Imagine two tribes meet at the river. Each tries to "empathize" with the other:

- Tribe A says, "It must be so hard, being less advanced than us."

- Tribe B replies, "We were just thinking how exhausting it must be for you to be so primitive."

Instead of bonding, they storm off, now *more* convinced of each other's inferiority.

That's empathy backfiring. It's not that the effort was bad—it's that without care, empathy can morph into pity, projection, or resentment.

In the chapters ahead, we'll explore how to make empathy work *with structure*: through listening, contact, and history's hard-won lessons. Because while empathy can backfire, it's still our best chance at bridging the tribal gaps.

Chapter 11: The Lost Art of Listening

Why We're Terrible at Listening

There's a joke that summarizes modern conversation:

"Are you listening to me?"
"What? No, I was just waiting for my turn to talk."

That's not far from the truth. Humans *think* they're good listeners, but research consistently shows we retain only about 25–50% of what we hear. The rest? Lost in the mental shuffle of rehearsing our next line, getting distracted, or planning dinner.

The Age of Multitasking

If you've ever nodded along to someone while simultaneously checking your phone, congratulations—you've committed a cardinal listening sin: **half-attention.**

Our brains aren't actually built for multitasking. When we pretend to do two things at once, we're really just switching rapidly between tasks. Which means when we're scrolling while "listening," we're not actually listening. We're glancing in and out of the conversation like tourists peeking through a window.

No wonder people feel unheard.

The Performance of Listening

Then there's **fake listening**—making just enough eye contact, dropping in the occasional "mm-hmm," while mentally drafting a grocery list.

Or worse: **competitive listening.** This is when you're not really hearing the other person's story, you're just waiting to pounce with your own, bigger, better story.

- Friend: "I'm so tired, I only got five hours of sleep last night."

- You: "Oh, that's nothing. I only got *three*! And my neighbor's dog kept me up, too."

What started as someone sharing their fatigue has now become a one-up contest.

Why We Rush to Fix

One reason we fail at listening is the **"problem-solver reflex."** When someone shares a struggle, we leap into advice mode:

- "You should just quit your job."

- "Have you tried yoga?"

- "You're overthinking it."

We do this because it feels efficient—fix the problem, move on. But here's the secret: most people aren't looking for solutions. They're looking for **understanding.** They want someone to say, "I hear you. That sounds hard."

Advice without empathy often feels like dismissal.

The Tribal Brain Twist

There's also a deeper reason listening is hard: our tribal brains.

When someone from our in-group talks, we're more willing to listen. When someone from an out-group speaks, our brains often filter their words through suspicion or defensiveness.

Instead of listening, we're scanning for disagreement, ready to counterattack. Which means we're not really hearing them—we're rehearsing our rebuttal.

It's not a conversation. It's pre-battle warm-up.

Part II: Empathetic Listening — The Secret Superpower

So, if humans are naturally bad at listening, what does *good* listening look like?

Psychologist Stephen Covey put it simply:

"Most people do not listen with the intent to understand; they listen with the intent to reply. Seek first to understand, then to be understood."

That's the heart of **empathetic listening.**

Listening as "Psychological Air"

Think of oxygen. You don't notice it when you have it, but when you're deprived, you panic.

Listening is the same. Most of the time, people don't consciously think, "I want to be heard." But when they *aren't* heard, they feel suffocated.

That's why Covey called empathetic listening **psychological air.** It doesn't solve the problem, but it makes space for breathing, healing, and dialogue.

The Mechanics of Empathetic Listening

So how does it work? Here are the building blocks:

1. **Give full attention.** Put the phone away. Make eye contact. Show with your body that you're present.

85

2. **Reflect, don't redirect.** Instead of turning the story back to yourself, mirror what they're saying:

   o   Them: "I'm exhausted from work."

   o   You: "Sounds like work is really draining you right now."

3. **Validate feelings.** You don't have to agree with their perspective to acknowledge it:

   o   "I can see why you'd feel that way."

   o   "That must be really tough."

4. **Hold space for silence.** Resist the urge to jump in. Sometimes the most powerful thing you can do is let a pause breathe.

A Conversation Makeover

Let's do a side-by-side:

- **Normal Listening:**
  Friend: "I've been so stressed."
  You: "Yeah, me too. Honestly, you should try meditating."

- **Empathetic Listening:**
  Friend: "I've been so stressed."
  You: "You've been carrying a lot lately. What's been the hardest part?"

The first response makes it about *you* and offers a quick fix. The second keeps the focus on *them* and invites deeper sharing.

Why It Works at the Tribal Level

Empathetic listening doesn't just help individuals—it reduces **tribal hostility.**

When rivals or out-group members feel genuinely heard, defenses soften. Research in conflict resolution shows that structured listening exercises (like repeating back what the other person said before replying) significantly reduce prejudice and hostility.

It doesn't mean agreement—but it does mean recognition. And recognition is often the first step to peace.

Humor Break: Things That Are *Not* Listening

- Nodding while secretly planning what to eat for dinner.

- Interrupting with, "That reminds me of this one time when *I…*"

- "Empathizing" by saying, "I know exactly how you feel. My cat once went through the same thing."

- Replying with a GIF instead of actual words.

Listening as Radical Humility

At its core, listening is humble. It's saying:

- "Your story matters as much as mine."

- "I don't need to fix you or win; I just need to understand."

In a world addicted to broadcasting—tweets, posts, hot takes—listening is almost countercultural. It slows us down. It reminds us that relationships aren't built on who talks the most, but on who hears the deepest.

The Big Lesson

If empathy is the muscle of connection, listening is the breath that keeps it alive.

- Without listening, empathy collapses into projection or pity.

- With listening, empathy becomes real recognition, even across tribal lines.

It sounds simple. But in practice, it's revolutionary.

Back to the Dinner Table

Imagine Uncle Joe again (yes, the touchdown guy). He's ranting about being underappreciated. Normally, the family rolls their eyes and changes the subject.

But this time, someone leans in and says:

- "It sounds like that touchdown was a really important moment for you. You want us to see how proud you are of it."

Uncle Joe stops. He blinks. For the first time, he feels… heard.

Does it solve the family drama? Maybe not. But it buys peace for one dinner. And sometimes, peace starts with a single person saying: *"I'm listening."*

Chapter 12: Contact Theory (Part I & II)

Part I: Allport's Big Idea

Let's start in 1954, with a Harvard psychologist named **Gordon Allport.** He was watching a world still smoldering from the ashes of World War II, riddled with segregation and prejudice, and asked a deceptively simple question:

"What would it take for groups who dislike each other to get along?"

His answer became one of the most influential ideas in social psychology: the **Contact Hypothesis.**

Contact, But Not Just Any Contact

Allport's insight was that simply throwing groups together doesn't automatically reduce prejudice. In fact, it often makes things worse.

Think of middle school dances: boys on one side, girls on the other, glaring across the room. Forced proximity? Yes. Successful integration? Absolutely not.

Allport argued that contact only works under specific conditions:

The Four Classic Conditions

1. **Equal Status:** Groups must meet on a level playing field. If one is clearly dominant, the weaker group's voices won't be heard.

   o Example: A workplace diversity initiative fails if the "minority representatives" are seated at the kids' table while executives dominate.

2. **Common Goals:** They must work toward something together. Not just sit side by side, but actually collaborate.

   o   Example: Rival schools working on a joint fundraiser.

3. **Intergroup Cooperation:** The goal has to require cooperation, not competition. If groups are pitted against each other, prejudice hardens.

   o   Example: Two sports teams playing each other? Rivalry increases. The same two teams rebuilding a community center? Prejudice decreases.

4. **Support of Authorities, Law, or Custom:** The larger system has to back the effort. If leaders, institutions, or social norms oppose the integration, contact collapses under pressure.

When these four conditions align, prejudice doesn't just soften—it can transform into friendship.

The "Robbers Cave" Experiment

One of the most famous demonstrations of this principle was the **Robbers Cave Experiment** in 1954.

Researchers brought two groups of boys to a summer camp. At first, the groups were kept apart and bonded internally. Then they were introduced through competition—sports, tug-of-war, even cabin inspections. The result? Rivalry, hostility, name-calling, even near-violence.

Then the researchers engineered **superordinate goals**—tasks that could only be achieved if both groups worked together. Like fixing the camp's broken water supply or pulling a stalled truck.

Slowly, the hostility melted. The boys began cooperating, eating together, even merging into a single group.

The lesson? Contact works—but only when structured around shared goals.

Part II: Putting Contact Into Practice

Allport's theory didn't stay in textbooks. It's been tested in classrooms, workplaces, neighborhoods, and even post-conflict societies. The results are mixed—but when done well, they're powerful.

Classrooms as Laboratories

Schools are one of the most common testing grounds for contact theory.

- **Desegregation in the U.S.:** When Black and white students were first integrated, results varied. In schools where Allport's conditions were met (equal status, supportive teachers, cooperative tasks), prejudice decreased. In schools where conditions were absent (segregation persisted in cliques, teachers didn't intervene), prejudice sometimes worsened.

- **International programs:** Student exchanges or joint projects across borders often foster empathy and cross-group friendships—again, when structured properly.

Classrooms show that contact isn't magic—it's design. The way the interaction is shaped determines whether it builds bridges or walls.

Dialogue Programs

In conflict-ridden societies, structured dialogue programs have used contact theory to remarkable effect.

- **Palestinian and Israeli youth programs** bring students together in neutral spaces, not to debate politics, but to share personal stories. The aim isn't to solve the conflict overnight—it's to humanize the "other."

- **Catholic and Protestant encounters** in Northern Ireland similarly focused on storytelling, music, and shared projects. Over time, the contact softened stereotypes and made space for reconciliation.

The key is structure: ground rules that promote listening, respect, and shared vulnerability. Without it, discussions spiral into defensive debates.

Role Reversal and Perspective Exercises

Some programs use **role reversal**—asking participants to literally take the other's role in a scenario.

For example, in community-police workshops, officers play the role of citizens facing stop-and-frisk, while citizens play the role of officers making split-second decisions.

The goal isn't pity—it's experiential understanding. And when combined with Allport's conditions, it often produces powerful breakthroughs.

Active Listening Pairs

Another application: structured "listening pairs." Two people from opposing groups take turns speaking for a set time while the other can only listen and reflect back. No rebuttals. No interruptions.

This format, used in mediation and therapy, harnesses the power of listening (from Chapter 11) and adds structure. It forces participants to step outside the tribal instinct to counterattack.

The result? Reduced hostility, increased trust, even among entrenched rivals.

When Contact Fails

Of course, contact can backfire when conditions aren't met:

- **Unequal status:** If one group dominates, the other feels tokenized.

- **Competition instead of cooperation:** If groups are forced to "share space" but compete for scarce resources, resentment spikes.

- **Lack of authority support:** If leaders don't back the effort, participants may fear backlash for crossing tribal lines.

Contact isn't a silver bullet. It's a delicate tool—powerful when used correctly, dangerous when misapplied.

Humor Break: "Contact" Gone Wrong

- Corporate retreat: "To build unity, we've paired Sales and HR for a three-legged race!" Result: bruises, insults, and two sprained ankles.

- School project: "Group work will teach cooperation." Translation: one kid does all the work while everyone else resents them.

- Family holiday: "Let's all sit together and talk it out." Three hours later, Aunt Linda is crying and someone has thrown cranberry sauce.

The Big Lesson

Allport's Contact Hypothesis isn't just a theory—it's a roadmap. When structured with equal status, cooperation, common goals, and institutional support, contact can chip away at centuries of prejudice.

But it requires intentionality. Just putting people in the same room isn't enough. You need the right recipe.

Back to the Campfire

Imagine two rival tribes meeting at the riverbank. If they just glare at each other, hostility grows. If they compete, hostility spikes.

But if they discover a broken bridge and realize it can only be rebuilt together? Slowly, hands meet, logs are lifted, and cooperation replaces rivalry.

That's contact theory in action: structured interaction that transforms "them" into part of "us."

Interlude #4: Thanksgiving Dinner Survival Guide

Thanksgiving: the annual American experiment in forced contact theory. Families gather, casseroles bake, and someone inevitably brings up politics at the table. By dessert, the turkey isn't the only thing carved up—it's also the relationships.

But don't worry. With a little science (and a lot of humor), you can survive—and maybe even enjoy—the tribal bonfire that is family dinner.

Step 1: Know Your Tribes

Every family gathering is really just a cluster of mini-tribes:

- **The Elders:** Guard the traditions. Will fight anyone who suggests ditching the stuffing recipe from 1957.

- **The Millennials/Gen Zs:** Armed with memes, plant-based diets, and Wi-Fi hotspots.

- **The Kids' Table:** Technically powerless, but highly disruptive. Their sugar highs dictate the evening's chaos.

- **The In-Laws:** Wild cards who may or may not survive initiation.

Recognizing the tribes is half the battle. The other half is pretending they're all one happy group called "family."

Step 2: Deploy Empathetic Listening

Remember Chapter 11? Listening is psychological air. At Thanksgiving, it's also the best fire extinguisher.

When Uncle Bob launches into a rant about taxes, don't fight back. Try this instead:

- "Sounds like you've been really stressed about the economy."

When Aunt Linda insists her essential oils can cure anything:

- "I can see why that feels meaningful to you."

You're not agreeing—you're validating. It's like sprinkling cinnamon on top of pumpkin pie: it makes everything easier to swallow.

Step 3: Establish Equal Status

Allport said contact requires equality. That means **no kids' table jokes**—at least not in earshot. Invite Cousin Jimmy to share his Roblox expertise. Hand Grandma the carving knife with reverence. Show the vegan cousin you took their diet seriously (even if the "Tofurky" looks suspiciously like a shoe).

When everyone feels respected, the hostility drops.

Step 4: Create Common Goals

Nothing unites warring factions like a shared mission. Examples:

- "We need to get the gravy on the table before it congeals."
- "Let's all team up to stop the dog from stealing the pie."
- "Nobody eats until we all take the family group photo."

Suddenly, Democrats, Republicans, vegans, and carnivores are allies—if only for five minutes.

Step 5: Redirect the Fire

If politics erupts, pivot to safer battlegrounds:

- "Who remembers the year the turkey caught on fire?"

- "What's the best bad Christmas gift you ever got?"

- "Let's rank the pies, gladiator-style."

Humor works like a circuit breaker. It resets the tribal brain.

Role Play Example

Here's a before-and-after using what we've learned:

- **Before (Typical Thanksgiving):**
  Uncle Joe: "This country's going downhill."
  Cousin Kayla: "That's because of your generation!"
  Grandpa: *bangs cane, yells about socialism.*
  → Everyone leaves early, cranberry sauce on the walls.

- **After (Survival Guide Version):**
  Uncle Joe: "This country's going downhill."
  Kayla: "You sound really worried about the future."
  Grandpa: "Back in my day, things were different."
  Kayla: "Tell me more about that."
  → Argument defused. Pass the stuffing.

Bonus Tips

- **Alcohol Moderation Rule:** Two glasses of wine = friendly bonding. Four glasses = reenactment of Robbers Cave experiment.

- **Seating Strategy:** Don't put Uncle Bob and Cousin Kayla next to each other. Do put the baby in the middle. Babies are empathy magnets.

- **Exit Strategy:** Have a "safe word" with your sibling. Example: "pass the gravy" = "please rescue me from this conversation."

The Big Idea

Thanksgiving dinner is basically a live-action simulation of contact theory. Equal status, common goals, empathetic listening, and humor can turn a potential food fight into a feast of connection.

It won't solve centuries of tribalism. But it might get you through dessert without flipping the table. And in family diplomacy, that counts as a peace treaty.

Chapter 13: History's Experiments (Part I & II)

Part I: South Africa & Northern Ireland

South Africa: Truth as Contact

For nearly half a century, South Africa was divided by apartheid: a legal system of racial segregation that disenfranchised the Black majority and privileged the white minority. When apartheid finally crumbled in the early 1990s, the country faced a question:

How do you move forward without tearing each other apart?

The answer was the **Truth and Reconciliation Commission (TRC)**, led by Archbishop Desmond Tutu.

The TRC wasn't perfect, but it was radical: instead of hiding atrocities under the rug, the nation dragged them into the open. Victims told their stories on public platforms. Perpetrators were encouraged to confess in exchange for amnesty. The whole country watched as wounds were voiced aloud.

It wasn't just about justice—it was about listening.

- Victims were heard.

- Perpetrators were humanized (without being excused).

- The nation practiced contact, not through small talk, but through painful storytelling.

The TRC showed that listening, even to horrors, can be a step toward coexistence.

Northern Ireland: The Good Friday Experiment

Northern Ireland, meanwhile, spent three decades (1968–1998) trapped in "The Troubles": a bitter conflict between Catholics (largely nationalist, seeking union with Ireland) and Protestants (largely unionist, seeking to remain with the UK). Bombings, assassinations, riots—it was tribalism weaponized.

The **Good Friday Agreement** of 1998 didn't magically erase hostility, but it established structures for power-sharing and dialogue.

The real breakthroughs, however, often came in small, everyday contact projects:

- Integrated schools where Catholic and Protestant children studied together.

- Youth programs where kids crossed neighborhoods once seen as no-go zones.

- Dialogue groups where former enemies told their stories face to face.

It wasn't kumbaya—it was messy, awkward, often tense. But the act of contact, structured with equal status and common goals, chipped away at stereotypes.

A Protestant teenager, after befriending a Catholic classmate, might still hold his political views—but now he knew someone on the "other side" as a person, not a faceless threat.

Shared Lesson from South Africa & Northern Ireland

Both cases underline Allport's principle: **contact alone isn't enough.** It has to be structured around truth, equality, and cooperation.

- South Africa leaned on **truth-telling** to humanize both victims and perpetrators.

- Northern Ireland leaned on **shared institutions and education** to foster equality.

Both proved that even after violence, human brains can stretch their tribal empathy—but only with careful scaffolding.

Part II: Rwanda & Lessons of Comparison

Rwanda: Justice by the Thousands

In 1994, Rwanda experienced one of the fastest genocides in history. In just 100 days, nearly a million people—mostly Tutsi—were slaughtered by extremist Hutu militias. When the killing stopped, the nation was left shattered: neighbor had killed neighbor, villages were drenched in trauma, and prisons overflowed with accused perpetrators.

The government faced an impossible question: how do you rebuild trust when the killers and the survivors still live side by side?

Their answer: the **Gacaca courts.**

These were community-based tribunals where perpetrators confessed and sought forgiveness, while survivors told their stories publicly. The goal wasn't just punishment—it was reintegration.

Like South Africa's TRC, the Gacaca courts relied on **truth-telling as contact.** But unlike South Africa, the process was hyper-local: it happened in villages, in front yards, under trees. Justice was communal.

It was imperfect. Some survivors felt retraumatized. Some perpetrators lied. But for many, the act of speaking and hearing began to stitch villages back together.

Comparing Models: TRC vs. Gacaca vs. Good Friday

Each case highlights different strengths and pitfalls:

- **South Africa (TRC):** National stage, cathartic storytelling, symbolic unity. Weak on material reparations.

- **Northern Ireland (GFA):** Institutional reform, education, and power-sharing. Slow, but gradually normalizing coexistence.

- **Rwanda (Gacaca):** Localized justice and reintegration. Pragmatic, but often painful for survivors.

The common denominator? **Contact plus structure.** Each nation created systems that forced tribes to face each other—not through violence, but through dialogue, ritual, or cooperation.

The Hard Reality

Let's be clear: none of these experiments were neat or perfect. Reconciliation is messy. People still carry trauma. Suspicion lingers. Political flare-ups still occur.

But compared to cycles of revenge, these structured contacts provided a fragile, but real, alternative path. They showed that tribal brains can, under the right conditions, expand their empathy circle—even after unthinkable violence.

Humor Break: Imagining Historical "Family Therapy"

Sometimes, reconciliation sounds like global-scale Thanksgiving therapy.

- South Africa: "Okay, everyone share what you did during apartheid. Be honest."

- Northern Ireland: "We'll take turns. No interrupting. Yes, that means you too, Gerry."

- Rwanda: "Confess your crimes to the whole village. No, you can't just say, 'oops.'"

Awkward? Painful? Yes. But sometimes, the only way forward is through the world's most uncomfortable group therapy session.

The Big Lesson

History's experiments show us two things:

1. **Tribal wounds can be addressed**—but only with structured systems of listening, contact, and shared goals. Left alone, they fester.

2. **There's no one-size-fits-all model.** Every context demands its own scaffolding. What matters is the principle: empathy, contact, and cooperation, backed by authority and structure.

Back to the Campfire

Picture again two rival tribes, but now not just glaring or cooperating on chores—they're sitting around a shared fire, telling their stories:

- "Here's what we did."

- "Here's what we suffered."

- "Here's how we can survive together."

The stories don't erase the pain. But they carve out a fragile space where enemies can become neighbors again.

That's what South Africa, Northern Ireland, and Rwanda tried: building new fires after old ones burned the world down.

Chapter 14: Toward an Enlightened Tribalism

The Good, the Bad, and the Tribal

Let's be honest: tribalism isn't all bad. It gave us family bonds, community rituals, and cheering sections at soccer games. It gave us language, culture, identity, and solidarity in the face of hardship.

The problem isn't **tribal belonging.** The problem is **tribal hostility.**

So what if we could keep the good parts—the sense of belonging, the loyalty, the shared meaning—while ditching the paranoia, prejudice, and occasional genocidal tendencies?

That's the dream of *enlightened tribalism.*

The Case for Tribal Belonging

Humans need tribes. Study after study shows that loneliness is as deadly as smoking 15 cigarettes a day. Belonging isn't optional—it's survival.

- **Support networks:** Tribes catch us when we fall.

- **Identity anchors:** Tribes tell us who we are.

- **Shared joy:** Tribes multiply our happiness through rituals, songs, meals, and celebrations.

If we tried to abolish tribal identity, we'd fail. People would just invent new tribes: fandoms, hobby groups, political parties, niche online communities.

So the challenge isn't to erase tribes—it's to make them wiser.

What "Enlightened" Looks Like

Enlightened tribalism is tribal belonging that is:

1. **Secure, not fragile.**

   o   Pride that doesn't demand constant validation.

   o   Confidence that doesn't collapse under difference.

2. **Inclusive, not exclusive.**

   o   Circles that welcome overlap.

   o   Identities that allow dual citizenship ("I'm both Irish *and* European," "I'm both Muslim *and* American").

3. **Purposeful, not paranoid.**

   o   Tribes united around creating, not fearing.

   o   Pride in contribution rather than superiority.

The Sports Analogy

Think of healthy sports rivalries. Fans cheer passionately for their teams, paint their faces, even cry when their side loses. But most know it's *just a game*.

Unenlightened tribalism: rioting when your team loses.
Enlightened tribalism: buying beers for rival fans after the game.

The trick is passion without paranoia.

How to Build Enlightened Tribes

1. Multiple Identities

The more identities you carry, the harder it is to dehumanize others. If you're a parent, a teacher, a hiker, and a Beyoncé fan, you overlap with a huge variety of people.

That overlap dilutes hostility. It makes it harder to reduce someone to "them" when you share at least one "us."

2. Shared Rituals Without Enemies

Tribes thrive on rituals—songs, meals, dances, holidays. But rituals don't need enemies.

- A town festival can celebrate heritage without mocking outsiders.

- A workplace can bond over team-building that doesn't revolve around beating another department.

- A fandom can celebrate their show without sending death threats to rival fans.

We don't have to strip away passion—we just have to decouple it from hostility.

3. Redefining Strength

In unenlightened tribes, strength means domination. In enlightened tribes, strength means resilience, creativity, generosity.

The strongest communities aren't the ones that shout loudest, but the ones that endure, adapt, and support their members through crises.

4. Leadership That Models Humility

Leaders set the tone. Narcissistic leaders create narcissistic tribes. Humble leaders create secure tribes.

When leaders admit mistakes, share credit, and emphasize common goals, tribes grow resilient rather than fragile.

5. Expanding the Circle

We may never erase in-group/out-group distinctions, but we can redraw the lines.

Instead of "my tribe vs. yours," we can frame superordinate identities:

- "We're all citizens of this city."

- "We're all part of this planet."

- "We're all fans of pie." (Arguably the most powerful identity.)

The point isn't to erase smaller tribes, but to nest them inside bigger ones.

Digital Tribes: Danger and Opportunity

Social media supercharges unenlightened tribalism: echo chambers, outrage mobs, online "wars." But it also shows the potential of enlightened tribalism.

- Online communities can mobilize aid for disaster victims within hours.

- Global fandoms can connect people across continents over shared passions.

- Social campaigns (#MeToo, #BlackLivesMatter, #ClimateStrike) can unite strangers into powerful movements for justice.

The same technology that feeds division can also fuel solidarity—if we design for it.

Humor Break: Spotting Enlightened vs. Unenlightened Tribes

- **Unenlightened tribe:** "We're the best. Everyone else is trash."

- **Enlightened tribe:** "We're great—and you're welcome to join us for nachos."

- **Unenlightened tribe:** "Our leader is flawless. Criticism = betrayal."

- **Enlightened tribe:** "Our leader forgot their speech notes. We laughed, then we helped them out."

- **Unenlightened tribe:** Starts wars.

- **Enlightened tribe:** Starts bake sales.

Case Studies in Enlightened Tribalism

- **Ubuntu in South Africa:** The philosophy of "I am because we are" emphasizes interconnectedness over rivalry. It's tribal identity that expands rather than shrinks.

- **The European Union (on good days):** Not perfect, but the attempt to create a "meta-tribe" of nations trading sovereignty for peace is an experiment in enlightened tribalism.

- **Disaster relief teams:** After hurricanes or earthquakes, people drop tribal labels to become "neighbors helping neighbors."

These aren't utopias. But they show that tribes can bond through **cooperation and care** instead of enmity.

The Big Lesson

We can't escape tribalism. But we can *choose what kind of tribes we build.*

- Unenlightened tribalism: fragile, paranoid, hostile.

- Enlightened tribalism: secure, generous, resilient.

The future depends on which path we take. Because tribalism isn't going away—it's the raw material of human society. The question is whether we mold it into bonfires that burn us, or hearths that warm us.

Back to the Campfire

Picture a new kind of fire. Not the small circle of "just us," glaring at "them" across the river. But a bigger circle, where the logs are heavy enough to need many hands, where the songs welcome many voices, and where pride doesn't require an enemy.

That's enlightened tribalism. Still tribal. Still human. But wiser than what came before.

Interlude #5: So, a Tribe Walks Into the Future...

Imagine humanity as one big group project (with legs, coffee addictions, and Wi-Fi issues). We've been fighting, reconciling, binge-watching, and occasionally burning things down for about 300,000 years. And now, we're standing together at the edge of tomorrow.

Here's the scene:

- **Team Humanity** is gathered around a giant metaphorical campfire.

- One faction insists on singing old songs loudly, slightly off-key.

- Another is livestreaming the fire to TikTok.

- A third is trying to use the flames to roast experimental plant-based marshmallows.

Everyone bickers. Someone drops a log. But despite the noise, we're still gathered *together.*

And that's the point: our species' story isn't one of harmony—it's one of learning how to stay in the same circle without storming off.

If the last chapters have shown anything, it's that we can't get rid of our tribal wiring. But we *can* laugh at it, work with it, and upgrade it.

The question is simple:
Will we keep using the fire to glare across the darkness?
Or will we use it to keep each other warm while we figure out the next verse of the song?

Either way, we'll need snacks.

Chapter 15: Survival of the Wisest

From Stone Tools to Supercomputers

Let's rewind one last time. Three hundred thousand years ago, our ancestors sat around small fires, worrying about mammoths and rival tribes. Their survival depended on sharp spears, sharper instincts, and loyalty to the 150 or so people they called "us."

Today, we sit around glowing screens instead of fires, worrying about climate change, artificial intelligence, and rival political tribes. Our survival no longer depends on spears, but on something much subtler: **wisdom.**

The irony is delicious. The brains that got us here—the tribal wiring that made us loyal, suspicious, and occasionally violent—are the very brains that could take us out. Survival is no longer about being the fittest. It's about being the *wisest*.

What We've Learned Along the Way

Let's quickly revisit the trail we've walked in this book:

- **We are tribal brains in modern bodies.** Our minds evolved for small, tight-knit groups, not for megacities and billion-person platforms.

- **Tribal instincts give us warmth and belonging.** They explain why we love sports, join fandoms, and cry at family movies.

- **But tribalism also breeds narcissism.** Groups demand recognition, see disrespect everywhere, and lash out at perceived slights.

- **Empathy is our superpower—but it's biased.** It flows freely for "us," trickles for "them," and sometimes backfires entirely.

113

- **Listening and structured contact are bridges.** They can transform hostility into coexistence—at Thanksgiving tables, in classrooms, and even between nations.

- **History shows reconciliation is possible.** South Africa, Northern Ireland, and Rwanda proved that with courage, structure, and painful honesty, humans can rebuild.

- **Enlightened tribalism is the future.** We don't need to erase tribes. We need to make them secure, generous, and inclusive.

Every step in that journey leads here: to the choice facing us now.

The Choice of Fires

Picture two fires.

At the first fire, the tribe huddles tightly, glaring out into the darkness. Their pride is fragile. Every rustle is a threat. Outsiders are mocked, feared, or attacked. The fire burns hot—but it burns small.

At the second fire, the circle is wider. Strangers are welcomed in. Stories flow across boundaries. Pride is secure, not brittle. The fire burns longer.

Humanity's future is about which fire we choose to gather around.

The Modern Challenges

Why does this matter now more than ever? Because the stakes have scaled up.

- **Climate challenges**: A global problem. One tribe cannot solve it alone.

- **Technology**: From nuclear weapons to AI, our inventions are powerful enough to destroy us—or save us—depending on how wisely we wield them.

- **Polarization**: Nations are splitting into rival tribes that see each other less as opponents and more as enemies.

- **Global pandemics**: Viruses don't care about borders, flags, or ideologies. But our responses too often do.

Our ancestors survived by banding together in small groups. We will survive only if we can learn to band together at scale.

Survival of the Wisest: What It Looks Like

So, what does wisdom look like in practice?

1. Humility Over Hubris

Fragile pride is dangerous. It makes groups lash out, retaliate, and spiral into conflict. Wisdom is secure enough to say:

- "We are strong, but we're not perfect."

- "We can be proud of who we are without tearing others down."

It's the difference between narcissistic groups and enlightened tribes.

2. Listening as Leadership

The wisest leaders aren't the loudest. They're the ones who listen deeply, reflect back, and make people feel heard.

Listening isn't soft. It's strategic. It defuses conflict, builds loyalty, and creates coalitions stronger than any single tribe.

3. Empathy, Upgraded

Our empathy circuits weren't designed for global crises. But through storytelling, contact, and deliberate practice, we can stretch them.

- Tell stories that humanize statistics.

- Build bridges through shared goals.

- Create rituals of solidarity that expand the circle of "us."

We don't need infinite empathy. We just need *enough empathy in the right places* to keep the fire burning.

4. Contact as a Default

Avoidance breeds suspicion. Contact breeds familiarity.

The more we create systems where people from different groups meet as equals—schools, workplaces, neighborhoods—the more we chip away at prejudice.

It won't erase conflict. But it makes coexistence possible.

5. Multiple Identities, Nested Tribes

The future belongs to people who can hold layered identities without cracking.

- "I'm a New Yorker, an American, and a human being."

- "I'm a Muslim, a scientist, and a fan of Marvel movies."

- "I'm part of my family tribe, my work tribe, and the tribe of people who think pineapple belongs on pizza."

Nested identities expand empathy. They make it harder to reduce someone to "them" when they also share a "us."

Humor Break: A Checklist for Enlightened Tribes

- Do you chant? ✓ (Rituals are fun.)

- Do you laugh together? ✓ (Bonding is healthy.)

- Do you believe your leader is perfect? ✗ (That's narcissism talking.)

- Do you invite outsiders to the nacho table? ✓ (That's enlightened tribalism.)

Lessons From History

South Africa, Northern Ireland, Rwanda—none of them achieved utopia. But all showed it's possible to step back from the brink.

The key wasn't erasing identity. It was building **systems of recognition and cooperation.**

If entire nations, scarred by blood and mistrust, can inch toward reconciliation, then surely Thanksgiving dinner—and maybe even Twitter—aren't beyond hope.

Wisdom as Evolution

Here's the evolutionary twist: survival used to be about sharp teeth and fast legs. Now, it's about **wise minds and cooperative hearts.**

The species that learns to manage its tribal fire—to keep it warm without letting it rage out of control—will outlast the rest.

In other words: it won't be survival of the fittest. It will be survival of the wisest.

Back to the Campfire One Last Time

So here we are, back at the fire. The logs are crackling. The circle is wide. Someone's off-key singing fills the night. Across from you sits someone who used to be a stranger. Maybe even a rival.

You pass them the bowl of food. They pass you the drink. And for a moment, the circle holds.

That's the vision of enlightened tribalism. That's the hope of survival of the wisest.

The question now is simple:
Will we choose small fires that scorch the earth?
Or will we choose bigger fires that light the way?

The future of our species depends on the answer.

Epilogue: The Fire, The Wi-Fi, and The Nachos

A Final Night by the Fire

Imagine, for a moment, that this book has been one long evening by the fire. We've told stories about our ancestors—hairy, wide-eyed, and worried about mammoths. We've poked fun at modern narcissistic tribes demanding frosted beer glasses at bars. We've laughed about Thanksgiving disasters, groaned about office politics, and cried a little over puppies.

And somewhere between the jokes and the science, we traced a single theme: **Humans are group projects with legs.**

We are brilliant, maddening, tribal creatures, constantly searching for belonging while tripping over our own fragile pride. And now, we face the greatest project of all: figuring out how to keep the circle wide enough to survive together.

A Look Back at the Journey

Let's glance in the rearview mirror one last time:

- We started with the **evolutionary roots**—brains wired for 150-person tribes.

- We explored the rise of **collective narcissism**—groups demanding constant recognition and erupting when they don't get it.

- We dove into **empathy**—our secret superpower, but one riddled with biases, gaps, and backfires.

- We practiced **listening**—the underrated art that feels like giving someone psychological oxygen.

- We learned about **contact theory**—the recipe for making enemies into neighbors through structured cooperation.

- We walked through **history's experiments**—South Africa, Northern Ireland, Rwanda—imperfect but inspiring.

- We dreamed of **enlightened tribalism**—keeping pride, joy, and ritual while discarding paranoia and hostility.

- And we ended with a call for **wisdom**—because survival is no longer about the fittest, but about the wisest.

That's the arc: from caveman campfires to the fragile global fire we tend today.

Lessons in Miniature (Or: Everything is Basically Thanksgiving)

If all of that feels overwhelming—global crises, psychological biases, historical traumas—don't worry. The same lessons apply at the dinner table.

- **Empathy gaps?** That's why you cry for the dog in the ASPCA ad but roll your eyes at your cousin's fourth divorce.

- **Collective narcissism?** That's why the family insists Grandma's stuffing recipe is the best in the universe and takes offense if you suggest adding garlic.

- **Contact theory?** That's why putting cousins from rival sides of the family on mashed potato duty together actually works.

The global is just the local with louder microphones. The tribal brain at the United Nations isn't so different from the tribal brain at Thanksgiving.

If we can practice patience, humility, and humor in our daily micro-tribes, we're rehearsing for the macro stage.

A Personal Note on Hope

It's easy, after tracing all this science and history, to feel bleak. The news cycle feeds us endless proof of tribal division: outrage mobs, political gridlock, international standoffs. You may wonder: can humans really get their act together?

But here's what keeps me hopeful: **we already do, every day.**

- Every time neighbors show up after a storm with hot soup.

- Every time strangers donate to disaster relief across the globe.

- Every time fans of rival teams end up laughing together in a bar (yes, it happens).

- Every time a family manages to get through a holiday meal without disowning each other.

These small fires matter. They prove that we're not just wired for hostility—we're wired for connection. We just need to practice stretching that connection beyond the easy circles.

Humor Break: The Future of Tribes

Picture the year 3024. Humans have colonized Mars. The old tribal instincts remain:

- The Martian settlers insist they're tougher than "Earth softies."

- Earth responds by bragging about oceans and fresh air.

- A third tribe forms around the Moon, declaring themselves "The Original Minimalists."

And yet… at the interplanetary summit, someone cracks a joke about pineapple on pizza. Everyone laughs, and suddenly the room feels lighter.

Some things never change. And maybe that's okay—because humor, like fire, is one of our oldest survival tools.

The Nacho Test

Here's one last silly rule of thumb for enlightened tribalism: **the nacho test.**

If your tribe's pride prevents you from sharing nachos with outsiders, you're in dangerous territory. If your pride *inspires* you to share nachos (and maybe brag about how your jalapeños are the best), you're on the path to wisdom.

It sounds ridiculous. But really, that's the crux: are we using our fire to hoard and exclude, or to welcome and share?

The Final Call

We've walked through evolutionary roots, narcissistic pitfalls, empathy hacks, historical lessons, and visions of enlightened tribes. But the truth is, none of it matters if it stays theoretical.

Every day, each of us makes tiny choices:

- Do I dismiss this stranger, or lean in with curiosity?
- Do I escalate this argument, or pause to listen?
- Do I retreat into "us vs. them," or redraw the circle wider?

The stakes may not feel global in the moment. But they add up. Billions of small tribal choices shape the fate of the species.

Survival of the wisest isn't just about governments and institutions. It's about us—daily, ordinary humans, deciding whether to be brittle or generous, hostile or hopeful.

Back to the Fire (One Last Time)

So here we are, together, at the end. The fire is lower now, the marshmallows mostly eaten, the songs winding down.

Look around. This is the tribe: messy, diverse, contradictory, sometimes infuriating, but ours. And if we can keep widening the circle—at dinner tables, in classrooms, online, across nations—we may just light a fire big enough to carry us through the dark.

Because in the end, humans are still group projects with legs. The question isn't whether we'll fight—that's inevitable. The question is whether we'll learn to fight *for each other,* not against.

The answer, I think, is up to us.

So, stoke the fire. Share the nachos. And let's see how far this tribe can go.

Bibliography

Core Foundations

Allport, Gordon W. *The Nature of Prejudice*. Reading, MA: Addison-Wesley, 1954.

Baumeister, Roy F., and Mark R. Leary. "The Need to Belong: Desire for Interpersonal Attachments as a Fundamental Human Motivation." *Psychological Bulletin* 117, no. 3 (1995): 497–529.

Dunbar, Robin. *How Many Friends Does One Person Need? Dunbar's Number and Other Evolutionary Quirks*. London: Faber & Faber, 2010.

Haidt, Jonathan. *The Righteous Mind: Why Good People Are Divided by Politics and Religion*. New York: Pantheon, 2012.

Sherif, Muzafer, O. J. Harvey, B. Jack White, William R. Hood, and Carolyn W. Sherif. *Intergroup Conflict and Cooperation: The Robbers Cave Experiment*. Norman: University Book Exchange, 1961.

Tajfel, Henri, and John C. Turner. "An Integrative Theory of Intergroup Conflict." In *The Social Psychology of Intergroup Relations*, edited by William G. Austin and Stephen Worchel, 33–47. Monterey, CA: Brooks/Cole, 1979.

Tutu, Desmond. *No Future Without Forgiveness*. New York: Image Books, 2000.

Neuroscience & Empathy Research

Decety, Jean, and Philip L. Jackson. "The Functional Architecture of Human Empathy." *Behavioral and Cognitive Neuroscience Reviews* 3, no. 2 (2004): 71–100.

Iacoboni, Marco. *Mirroring People: The Science of Empathy and How We Connect with Others*. New York: Picador, 2009.

Singer, Tania, and Claus Lamm. "The Social Neuroscience of Empathy." *Annals of the New York Academy of Sciences* 1156, no. 1 (2009): 81–96.

Zaki, Jamil. *The War for Kindness: Building Empathy in a Fractured World.* New York: Crown, 2019.

Sociology of Digital Tribes & Polarization

Bail, Christopher A. *Breaking the Social Media Prism: How to Make Our Platforms Less Polarizing.* Princeton, NJ: Princeton University Press, 2021.

Pariser, Eli. *The Filter Bubble: What the Internet Is Hiding from You.* New York: Penguin Press, 2011.

Sunstein, Cass R. *#Republic: Divided Democracy in the Age of Social Media.* Princeton, NJ: Princeton University Press, 2017.

Turkle, Sherry. *Alone Together: Why We Expect More from Technology and Less from Each Other.* New York: Basic Books, 2011.

Vosoughi, Soroush, Deb Roy, and Sinan Aral. "The Spread of True and False News Online." *Science* 359, no. 6380 (2018): 1146–1151.

Cultural & Contemporary Perspectives

Cialdini, Robert B. *Influence: The Psychology of Persuasion.* New York: Harper Business, 2006.

Levine, Robert A., and Donald T. Campbell. *Ethnocentrism: Theories of Conflict, Ethnic Attitudes, and Group Behavior.* New York: Wiley, 1972.

Pink, Daniel. *Drive: The Surprising Truth About What Motivates Us.* New York: Riverhead Books, 2009.

Glossary

Altruism – Acting to help others, sometimes at a cost to oneself. In tribal settings, altruism often strengthens bonds within the group.

Algorithmic Bonfire – A playful phrase in the book describing how social media algorithms amplify outrage and tribal conflict, much like throwing gasoline on a campfire.

Collective Narcissism – When a group (nation, religion, political party, sports team, etc.) believes it is exceptional and demands constant recognition, reacting angrily when that recognition is not given.

Contact Hypothesis – A theory by Gordon Allport suggesting that prejudice between groups can be reduced if certain conditions are met, including equal status, common goals, cooperation, and support from authority.

Dunbar's Number – The idea, proposed by anthropologist Robin Dunbar, that humans can maintain stable social relationships with about 150 people. Beyond this number, relationships become harder to sustain.

Empathy – The ability to understand and share the feelings of another. In the book, it's described as humanity's "emotional Wi-Fi."

Empathy Gap – The tendency for people to feel more empathy for those in their own group (or for puppies and fictional characters) than for distant strangers.

Enlightened Tribalism – A hopeful vision for the future: keeping the sense of belonging, pride, and ritual from tribal life, but without hostility or paranoia toward outsiders.

In-Group – The people we see as part of "us," usually our family, community, or social group.

Mirror Neurons – Specialized brain cells that fire both when we perform an action and when we observe someone else performing it. They are thought to be linked to empathy and imitation.

Out-Group – The people we see as "them," often treated with suspicion, prejudice, or hostility.

Psychological Air – A term popularized by Stephen Covey to describe the feeling of being listened to. Just as people need oxygen, they also need to feel heard.

Robbers Cave Experiment – A famous 1954 psychology study showing how quickly intergroup conflict can escalate—and how cooperation on shared goals can reduce hostility.

Superordinate Goals – Objectives that require cooperation from multiple groups to achieve, often used to reduce conflict between rivals.

Tribal Brain – The evolutionary wiring that makes humans identify with "us" versus "them," favor our group, and distrust outsiders.

Truth and Reconciliation Commission (TRC) – A restorative justice body established in South Africa after apartheid to uncover past human rights abuses and promote reconciliation.

Ubuntu – A Southern African philosophy meaning "I am because we are," emphasizing interconnectedness and shared humanity.